Notions

Notions

Over
50
Great
Gadgets
You Can't
Live Without

The Taunton Press

Publisher: Jim Childs
Acquisitions editor: Jolynn Gower
Assistant editor: Sarah Coe
Editorial assistant: Meredith DeSousa
Copy editor: Suzanne Noel
Cover designer: Susan Fazekas
Interior designer/layout artist: Susan Fazekas
Illustrator: Ron Carboni

Taunton
PUBLICATIONS

for fellow enthusiasts

Printed in Malaysia
10 9 8 7 6 5 4 3 2 1

The Taunton Press, Inc.
63 South Main Street, P.O. Box 5506, Newtown, CT 06470-5506
e-mail: tp@taunton.com

Distributed by Publishers Group West

Library of Congress Cataloging-in-Publication Data

Notions : over 50 great gadgets you can't live without.
        p. cm.
    ISBN 1-56158-415-0
    1.Sewing—Equipment and supplies. 2.Notions (Merchandise)

TT715 .N68 2000
646'.1—dc21   00-037393

acknowledgments

The idea for this book came about with a visit to the Husqvarna Viking home office in Cleveland. Some colleagues and I were meeting with Theresa Robinson, notions buyer for Husqvarna Viking. She suggested a book on notions, with the information based on a class she teaches at sewing shows called "Notions Commotion." Needless to say, I loved the idea and so did all the contributors who participated in this project.

We at The Taunton Press would like to thank Theresa Robinson for sharing her wonderful idea and generously giving us the opportunity to publish this book. Also, we would like to thank the contributors who shared their knowledge, enthusiasm, and time to create this helpful guide.

—*Jolynn Gower, Acquisitions Editor*

contents

contributors

CAROL AHLES has taught sewing techniques to over 5,000 students. A lifelong sewer and former owner of a sewing-machine dealership/fabric shop, she is a frequent contributor to *Creative Needle* and *Threads* magazines, and is the author of *Fine Machine Sewing*. She currently lives in Houston, Texas.

DODY BAKER is an internationally recognized teacher of heirloom sewing. An instructor of the Beginning Heirloom School at the Martha Pullen School of Art Fashion in Huntsville, Alabama, she also teaches Mastery of the Pleater and Smocking. Dody is a freelance heirloom teacher and has had numerous articles published in *Sew Beautiful* magazine. She currently resides in Huntsville, Alabama.

SANDRA BETZINA is the host of 255 *Sew Perfect* television shows on HGTV. In addition to her syndicated sewing column, Sandra is a regular contributor to *Vogue Pattern Magazine, Threads,* and *Australian Stitches;* the creator of *Power Sewing* books and videos; and the author of *Fabric Savvy, No Time to Sew, More Power Sewing,* and *Power Sewing Step-by-Step*. She conducts seminars nationally and internationally, as well as week-long workshops in San Francisco.

CARI CLEMENT became involved in the needlework industry when *Family Circle* published her first sweater design. Since then, she's designed sweaters for most of the leading knitting magazines and yarn companies, owned a yarn store, and also designed her own line of knitwear. She is president of Bond America, a manufacturer of needlework tools. Cari lives in the Adirondack Mountains in northern New York.

CLOTILDE is the author of *Sew Smart* and the president of her own mail-order sewing-notion catalog, Clotilde. Her career in the fabric/sewing industry began at 20th Century Fox Studios in the wardrobe department. Since then, Clotilde has shared her sewing knowledge through books, lectures, a cable TV program, and guest appearances on PBS sewing shows.

BARBARA DECKERT has more than 30 years of sewing experience and is a custom clothier. She is a frequent contributor to *Threads* and *Sew News* magazines and also writes regularly for the national newsletter *PACC News*. In addition, she also teaches seminars for custom clothiers.

EMMA GRAHAM is a well-known sewing enthusiast who takes her love of fabric to heart. Emma has worked professionally in fashion design, custom doll clothing, quilting, and patternmaking, and has owned her own dressmaking and home-decorating business. Emma and her husband, Don, an engineer, invented the Fasturn, and she has been teaching its use ever since. Today they own a retail store, Fasturn Junction, in Medford, Oregon.

JAN GRIGSBY worked for several years at G Street Fabrics in Rockville, Maryland. She is the former editor of *McCall's Quilting* magazine and is also the former vice president of marketing for Bonfit America, Inc. Jan lives in California.

SUE HAUSMANN is the host of *America Sews,* a public-television series. As senior vice president for a major sewing-machine manufacturer, she oversees the education and training programs for consumers and is intensely involved with consumer-motivation programs and new-product development. Sue has more than 19 books to her credit, including the *America Sews* books and *Sew Fast, Faster, Fastest*.

GALE GRIGG HAZEN began her career in the sewing industry in a sewing-machine dealership, selling and repairing machines. Today she is a nationally known sewing, fitting, and machine expert. In addition to being a regular contributor to *Threads* magazine and *Sew News,* she is also the author of several books, including *The Owner's Guide to Sewing Machines* and *Fantastic Fit for Every Body*.

SUSAN KHALJE is the director of the Couture Sewing School, which she founded in 1993. She writes for *Threads* magazine and is the author of *Bridal Couture* and *Linen and Cotton*.

LINDA LEE is the owner of The Sewing Workshop in San Francisco, a sewing and design school for hobby and professional sewers and artists, and Linda Lee Design Associates, an interior-design firm specializing in commercial and residential design and space planning. She is a frequent guest on HGTV's *Today at Home* and is also the author of three books: *Sewing Edges and Corners*, *Scarves to Make*, and *Sewing Luxurious Pillows*.

CONNIE LONG is an avid sewer who teaches a variety of sewing classes on all aspects of clothing construction. She is a frequent contributor to *Threads* magazine, and her most recent book is *Sewing with Knits*.

LYLA MESSINGER designs patterns for her company, L. J. Designs. She travels internationally, sharing ideas to help individuals create garments that reflect their personality. Lyla has written many booklets featuring her novel approach to creating unique garments, which, along with her techniques, are often featured in popular sewing magazines.

KAREN MORRIS, of Boston, Massachusetts, works as a freelance writer, designer, and health-care consultant, and is a contributing editor of *Threads* magazine. For 10 years, she designed her own line of knitwear, performing every job from design, marketing, and production to shopping the market and writing invoices. She has also taught classes at sewing conventions.

MARY MORRIS's only formal sewing training was an eighth-grade sewing class and two years working in the costume shop at The Catholic University of America. Later, she became deeply involved in designing and creating costumes for a youth ballet company. Currently, in addition to being the book buyer for G Street Fabrics in Rockville, Maryland, she also teaches classes and has authored a book, *Every Sewer's Guide to a Perfect Fit*.

MARY LIBBY NEIMAN has been designing and teaching with textiles for over 25 years. She began her career manufacturing and designing women's fashion accessories and, at the college level, has taught and lectured on spinning. Today, she works at her own company, On the Surface, which offers embellishment fibers and manufacturers' specialty threads and tools for the sewing and craft industries.

SYL PEARSON has been associated with the fabric industry for over 25 years in a variety of roles, including fabric buyer, store manager, salesperson, designer, instructor, and trade-show demonstrator. She currently works as a design consultant/demonstrator for Clover Needlecraft, Inc. Syl resides in Maple Grove, Minnesota, with her husband, daughter, and two cats.

THERESA ROBINSON has been involved in the sewing industry in a variety of roles, including pattern designer, quilt maker, and notions exporter, as well as author and teacher. She is currently a notions marketing specialist for Husqvarna Viking.

SANDY SCRIVANO is a design artist of eclectic interest. She currently has an active business, Sandy Scrivano Designs, that includes gallery and custom private work. She is a regular contributor to *Threads* magazine and has written several books, including *Sewing with Leather and Suede*. She also teaches regularly at sewing schools, guilds, colleges, conferences, and retreats.

GAYLE STARBUCK's introduction to the world of sewing came from scrap bags full of silks, lace, and ribbons, along with encouragement from her grandmother. Her work has appeared in *Crafts* and *Arts and Crafts* magazines, and she designed Bonfit's *Artistry with Elastic* and *Ribbon* books. Gayle currently does design work from her California home.

PAT WELCH was part owner of a design shop in Boulder, Colorado, for 15 years. She now travels frequently as part of her job as a national educator for Sulky of America. *The Sewing Professional* named her one of the sewing stars of the industry.

ANNA ZAPP is a professional dressmaker who, together with Nora Cray, invented the ergonomic sewing system. She has designed everything from handmade western shirts to wedding and evening gowns to business suits. She currently owns a couture design studio and lives in Colorado.

introduction

While you may be able to live without *every* wonderful notion included in this guide, you'll have a difficult time choosing, as they all make sewing easy and fun. Whether you're an avid quilter or an enthusiastic embellisher, there's a notion here that will help improve your sewing skills and encourage your creativity. While this book certainly doesn't include every notion, it's a good start—with over 50 favorite, tried-and-true items from some of the best and most experienced educators and sewing enthusiasts around.

We asked 23 sewing experts from all over the country to share their favorite notions and how they use them. In some cases, these sewers also included instructions for a project that can be made using the notion. The final list that resulted from our query covers a variety of sewing topics, including Creating Embellishments, Cutting and Marking Tools, Pressing Aids, Stabilizing and Structuring Aids, Machine Accessories, Needles and Threads, and Aids for Precision Sewing.

This list says a lot about sewing today: Most notably, embellishing continues to be a hot topic for sewers, evident in the amount of material devoted to this topic in sewing books and articles, and it's an area that is of interest to every kind of sewer. Choosing the basic fabric and pattern for your projects involves a certain level of creativity, but today's broad range of embellishing techniques offers an even more expressive way to create unique, personal projects.

We hope you enjoy this book and find many useful products that help you in your sewing. If you can't find the notion in your local fabric store, we have included an extensive resource list in the back of the book. Many of these sources have a mail-order service to accommodate customers all over the United States and Canada.

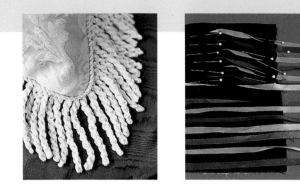

creating

Embelli

Embellishments are a great way to customize and accent everything from garments to home-decorating projects. Without the right tools, many of these techniques can be time-consuming, difficult, or both. With just a small initial investment, you can create custom details that will be so easy to do, you'll be adding them everywhere! In this section, you'll find notions that can help you create embellishments quickly and accurately, and with fabulous professional results.

Imagine the creative possibilities of creating the motif for a magnificent scarf using burned-out velvet, or customizing a fabric to fit the pattern pieces of a garment you're making. Even something as quick and easy as a swipe with a specialty-edge rotary cutter can turn a fleece or leather garment into something exciting. From perfect, even pleats to custom cording, you can get the results you want in your very own sewing room.

shments

Specialty-Edge Rotary Cutter

Sandy Scrivano

R otary cutters, with their wheel-shaped blades and extremely sharp edges, are helpful tools to cut through fabric; they are used with a special cutting board, which the blades cannot damage. In addition to plain rotary cutters, specialty-edge rotary cutters are also available. They are a good way to add design interest to garments and accessories made with nonraveling materials, such as leather, suede, Polarfleece, melton, vinyl, Ultrasuede, and Ultraleather.

The nonraveling characteristic of these materials requires no edge finish, so the cut edges themselves become part of the overall design. Using a rotary cutter with either a wavy edge or a zigzag blade is a quick way to create these interesting edges in a continuous line; it also helps eliminate breaks from regripping that may occur when using scissors for this purpose. My favorite brand is Olfa, because of its good blade quality and durability.

USING A SPECIALTY-EDGE ROTARY CUTTER

For the greatest success, hold the rotary cutter perpendicular to the surface to be cut and apply continuous, even pressure as the cut is made. You may want to use a straightedge as a guide. If your blade is sharp, there will

be no skips along the cut line. These blades do not have sharpeners, so when you see skips, it's time to change to a new blade.

Decorative edges on leather garments

Of the nonraveling materials mentioned previously, leather and suede in particular are very popular in the fashion world. Despite what you might think, garments made of these fabrics are surprisingly affordable when you sew them yourself. To add your own personal touch, you can use specialty-edge rotary cutters for lapped seams and decorative-edge finishes on leather skirts, tops, and jackets.

To make the garment assembly go quickly, I use single-layer construction, which means no facings, interfacings, linings, or finishing

of seam allowances. Closures are eliminated or simplified. To make this type of construction work, choose a simple pattern with few or no shaping darts, princess seams, welt or in-seam pockets, vents, pleats, and the like. Patterns that are designed for use with fleece fabrics work well for single-layer construction.

Because constructing a leather garment is quite easy, I find that I have more time to spend on the decorative details. For the garment's exposed edges, experiment with the wavy and zigzag rotary cutter blades that are available. These blades can be used to showcase outer, seam, and pocket edges. Simply cut out the leather, lap the seams once, and stitch the seam.

Whatever type of garment you're working on, whether it's leather or another nonraveling material, specialty-edge rotary cutters offer an opportunity to embellish without adding lots of time or effort.

Perfect Pleater

Clotilde

T he technique of pleating is over 100 years old. Although pleating was initially done by hand or with a board (I have one trademarked by Milton J. Bradley in 1883), many types of hand-held machines were developed over the years.

Today's version is the Perfect Pleater, a device with a series of louvers into which you tuck fabric. By changing the direction of the fabric and skipping louvers, you can literally turn even ugly fabric into a work of art.

The original Perfect Pleater is an 8-in. by 11-in. piece of cardboard covered with fabric, which has been permanently tucked into ¼-in.-wide louvers that are 11 in. long. The "return," or depth of each louver, is always ⅜ in. Therefore, when making

pleats that are ½ in. or ¾ in. wide, for example, the right side has only a ⅜-in. return, which saves fabric and bulk.

Variations of the original Perfect Pleater include the Extra-Long Perfect Pleater, which has the same-width louvers but is 22 in. long, and the Skirt Perfect Pleater, which is 13 in. by 27 in. long. The latter has ¾-in.-wide louvers that have 1⅜-in. return to provide the fullness needed for a skirt. With the Skirt Perfect Pleater, you can create ¾-in.-, 1½-in.-, 2¼-in.-, or 3-in.-wide pleats, but the return is always only 1⅜ in. Together, these pleaters allow unlimited variations.

USING THE PERFECT PLEATER

The Perfect Pleater is very easy to use; it's a simple matter of tucking the fabric properly and then steaming the pleats in place. One yard of fabric makes 10 in. of ¼-in. pleats, 17 in. of ½-in. pleats, 22 in. of ¾-in. pleats, and 24 in. of 1-in. pleats.

1 Before beginning to pleat, relax the louvers by rolling the board back against itself. Place the pleater on an ironing board with the louvers opening up away from you.

2 Extend a seam allowance beyond the edge of the pleater, which makes fabric removal easier when you're finished pleating. Hold the fabric in

place by pinning it to the pleater board along the side closest to you. This helps to keep the fabric straight.

3 Begin tucking at the center and work out to the sides, as shown. Working from the center out helps keep the fabric on grain for a more professional look. You may need to use a credit card or a ruler to push the fabric all the way down into each louver.

4 With your iron at a cotton setting, press the fabric in the pleater to set the pleats. Using a press cloth that has been dipped in a mixture of 1 part white vinegar to 9 parts water, press the tucks into place. It's important to allow the pleats to cool before removing them from the pleater, as this helps to set them.

5 Before removing the fabric from the pleater board, remove the anchor pins and machine-stitch the extended seam allowance.

> **Tip**
>
> To create no-sew tucks, simply tuck the fabric right side down into the pleater. After pressing but before removing, fuse the entire wrong side of the tucked fabric with a lightweight fusible tricot interfacing. Roll the pleater back against itself to release the now-tucked fabric, and you have perfect no-sew tucks.

6 Pull the fabric gently from the board. The pleats are securely held in place along one edge. If you need additional help in holding the pleated fabric together, use strips of Wash-A-Way Wonder Tape or Res-Q Tape.

To pleat continuous yards of fabric, take the last pleat made and insert it into the first louver. Continue pleating, then press and repeat the process.

For permanent pleats, use a 50/50 poly/cotton blend or all-polyester fabric. While the fabric is in the pleater, press it with the Rajah Press Cloth. It's the magic of polyester, the chemicals in the Rajah Press Cloth, and heat that make permanent pleats; all other fabrics require repeat pressing to hold the pleats.

To create scallops, use any lace, ribbon, or fabric that has both edges clean-finished. (For fabric, cut cross-grain strips 2 in. to 3 in. wide and serge both edges to clean-finish each side.) Simply insert the lace into three louvers. While holding these in place, angle the lace upward at a 45-degree angle and pleat three louvers "up the hill." Straighten the lace and pleat three louvers straight, then angle the lace down at a 45-degree angle to pleat three more louvers "down the hill." Again, straighten the lace and pleat three more louvers. Repeat the steps as desired, then press and let cool.

In this case, since it's not possible to machine-stitch before removing the fabric from the pleater, hold the strips in place with Res-Q Tape or Wash-A-Way Wonder Tape before removing the fabric for machine-stitching later. Once it has been removed, machine-stitch above the tape—never through it—to hold the pleats securely in place.

CLOTILDE'S TWISTED RIBBON VEST

Materials

2 yd. to 3 yd. of silk or polyester satin, depending on the size of the vest
Fourteen 3½-yd. spools of double-faced ¼-in. satin ribbon
Vest pattern of your choice
Fusible tricot interfacing

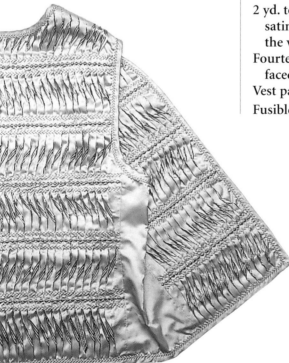

1 Place fabric right side down on the pleater. Tuck fabric into every other louver to create ½-in. pleats. Press the tucks into place using a press cloth dampened in a solution of 9 parts water and 1 part white vinegar and wrung out. Remove the press cloth, and let the fabric cool.

2 With the fabric still in the pleater, place the fusible tricot interfacing, fusible side down, onto the fabric. Fuse in place. Continue pleating and fusing until the required pleated yardage has been made. Remove the fabric once it has thoroughly cooled, about 2 minutes. The pleated fabric is now tucked (permanently placed) as a result.

3 Mark the stitching lines 3½ in. apart across the right side of the tucked fabric, but don't stitch. Use Clo-Chalk or purple vanishing pen for marks that will disappear after 48 hours. Each marked line will be turned and stitched in the opposite direction of the line above it.

4 Beginning at the top of each tuck, position a length of ribbon in one tuck at a time, securing it with a pin. Pull the ribbon from underneath the tuck, roll it over the tuck, and pin it in place under the same tuck, as shown, at the 3½-in. marked line. Continue by drawing the ribbon from

Tip

To save time creating a hem or clean-finishing the hem edge, simply fold the fabric in half. Then pleat the doubled layers of fabric. The edges will be finished for a lovely ruching, curtain tieback, or pleated edging for a skirt or hand towel.

under the tuck and rolling it over the reversed tuck. Continue this "zigzag" up, over, and under twisting motion along the entire length of the tuck. When all of the ribbon/tucked fabric has been pinned, stitch along each line in the direction of the tucks.

5 Lay your vest pattern onto the ribbon/tucked fabric. Trace around the pattern piece, and mark the shape onto your ribbon/tucked fabric.

6 Before cutting out the fabric, staystitch around the pattern outline. If you cut before staystitching, the ribbons will unwind. For less bulk, do not use tucks or ribbons under the arms. Note: Tucks at the bottom of the vest front should face away from the center front (going toward the side seam). Back tucks should all face in the same direction.

7 Line the entire vest to cover the fusible interfacing. Bind all edges with self-fabric bias binding.

4

Smocking Pleater

Dody Baker

$\mathcal{A}$ smocking pleater is designed to place pleats in fabric to prepare for smocking. Smocking pleater characteristics differ from one brand to another, based on four significant features:

- spacing of the needles, which is important to know when pleating for picture smocking;

- pleat depth, which can be unequal on some pleaters, resulting in different lengths of stitches on opposite sides of the pleated fabric;

- whole- and half-space counts, which will depend on what you're making;

- needle types, which are not always interchangeable. When ordering needles, always identify the pleater by brand name.

I like to use Dr. Joe's Pleater because it has 24 whole-space rows and 48 half-space rows, 48 high-quality needles, a screwdriver, and a thread holder with space for 24 bobbins. Its large end openings make for easy pleating, and a white Lucite base makes threading the needles easy as well.

Current Available Brands		
Brand	Rows	Spacing (between rows)
Dr. Joe's Pleater	24	⅜ in.
Amanda-Jane	24	1 cm
Little Amanda	16	⅜ in.
The Super Amanda	24	1 cm
Pullen	16	⅜ in.
Sally Stanley	24	1 cm

PARTS OF THE SMOCKING PLEATER

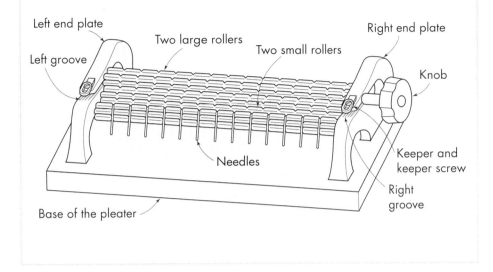

Left end plate

Left groove

Two large rollers

Two small rollers

Right end plate

Knob

Needles

Keeper and keeper screw

Right groove

Base of the pleater

A smocking pleater works by sending fabric through its gears, forming pleats that are fed onto curved needles located inside the gear structure. The pleats are then pulled off the end of the needle shank onto strong quilting threads. The simple machine performs what used to be an arduous task of ironing dots onto fabric and picking up each dot with a needle and thread to form the pleats.

The parts of a typical pleater are noted in the above figure.

USING A SMOCKING PLEATER

A smocking pleater can be adapted to the needs of each specific project. It's best to do a few practice runs to get familiar with the different results you can achieve simply by varying the space of the needles. Here are some exercises to give you a feel for the correct way to use the pleater.

Materials

A spool of quilting thread (bright blue, orange, or white)
Dental floss threader or a needle/looper threader
Scissors
An empty film canister
Screwdriver
6-in. by 12-in. piece of striped fabric
6-in. by 12-in. piece of plaid fabric
¼-in. dowel
Long tweezers
Wash-away marking pen
Waxed paper

1 To prevent the pleater needles from tumbling out, tilt up the front part of the pleater on a thin book. Remove the small top roller according to your pleater instructions, then remove all the needles. Depending on how wide you want your pleats, count out the number of needles that you need and place the remaining needles (eye first) into an empty film canister.

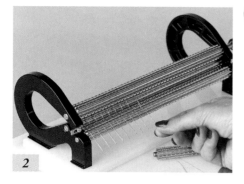

2

2 Place the first needle in the first vertical groove nearest to the left end plate. To prevent damage to the point of the needle, insert it "elbow" down into the selected vertical groove on the bottom small roller. Let the point of the needle fall gently into position. Continue adding needles according to the number of rows required, as discussed in your pleater instructions. Then carefully replace the small top roller and secure it.

3 Place the pleater on a flat surface. To keep the top raw edge of the fabric aligned with the correct needle space, make what I call a magic mark in an empty groove on the large top roller with a quilting thread that is a contrasting color to your rollers. To create this magic mark, thread an 8-in. piece of quilting thread through the loop of the threader. Place the tapered end of the threader into the first whole space to the right of the last needle. Turn the pleater handle toward the back of the pleater.

4 Before pleating, prepare the fabric. Wash fabrics that are too stiff from sizing to soften them. For soft, sheer fabrics, add body by starching and ironing. Trim away selvages that may break pleater needles.

5 Mark the center of the fabric on both sides with thread or a wash-away marking pen. Next, you'll need to determine which side of the fabric faces up when fed into your pleater. All pleaters are different (even within the same brand); some require the wrong side of the fabric to face up, while others require it to be right side up. Ultimately, the long stitches should end up on the wrong side of the fabric, once pleated. (Remember the rule this way—"long is wrong.") Use a small sample of fabric that has a definite wrong side and pleat a test strip.

6 Roll the fabric onto a dowel. For thick fabrics or large garments, roll the fabric so that the edges are uneven, forming a cone shape. Even though the fabric will come off the dowel at an angle, insert it so that the straight of grain enters the pleater evenly.

7 Place the dowel through both end plates. The fabric may not extend through the opening of the right end plate; in most cases it will pass through only the left end plate. If your fabric is so long that it extends off the end of your dowel, simply shorten the length of fabric by folding the edge onto itself so that it does not hang off the end of the dowel.

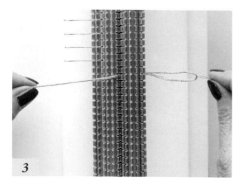

3

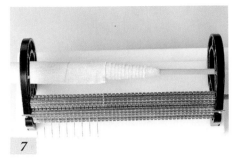

7

1

PLEATING THE FABRIC

For the exercises below, thread eight needles. If your pleater does not have a thread holder or is not mounted to a thread holder, cut quilting thread for each needle. Until you are comfortable with the correct amount to cut off, I recommend at least 2 yd. You can thread the needles from either the top or the bottom, but be consistent. As you complete the threading, leave a 6-in. tail of thread at each needle eye.

Experience is the best way to perfect the art of pleating. The following exercises will introduce you to the techniques for various types of projects.

Learning proper feed

Pleating off grain is a common problem for the beginner. This exercise uses striped fabric in order to observe feeding on the straight of grain.

1 Prepare the pleater and striped fabric, then thread eight needles as directed previously. Facing the back-

 Half-space needles can be identified easier if threaded with a second color. If your pleater is mounted on a black base, placing a white paper under the needles will make threading the needles easier.

side of the pleater, lay the fabric into the slot between the two large rollers. The raw edge of the fabric must be aligned to the magic mark. It is critical that the fabric begins feeding evenly into the pleater.

2 While supporting the fabric, carefully turn the large top roller (not the knob) slightly with your fingers, just enough to grip the edge of the fabric between the two large rollers. If you choose to pleat with the back of the pleater facing you, this gives you an excellent view of how the fabric is entering the pleater. The needles should enter the fabric evenly along the edge of one stripe.

3 Begin pleating by turning the knob three rotations away from the needles. Pull the pleated fabric off the needles onto the thread to prevent accidental unthreading. Since there is no pressure on the fabric that passes through the slots in the end plates, gently pull the fabric toward the needle side using your free hand (see the photo on p. 18). (Pulling sideways will distort the alignment of the raw edge with the magic mark.)

If one end of a stripe is feeding into the roller before the rest of the stripe, grasp that part of the fabric and dowel and hold firmly while turning the knob. This will allow the lagging section to catch up and get back on grain. This is the only time you should have your hands on the fabric and

1 Prepare the pleater and plaid fabric, then thread eight needles, as directed above.

2 Line up the raw edge of the fabric with the magic mark. Select a roller groove that aligns with a dominant vertical line in the plaid, and place a second magic mark in that groove.

dowel while pleating; otherwise, skipped or Y pleats can occur.

4 When the needles are about two-thirds full of pleated fabric, or the knob becomes hard to turn, gently pull the pleats off the needles and down onto the guide threads. Keep the pleats packed together. Continue pleating, maintaining the alignment of the raw edge with the magic mark, keeping the grain line straight, and guiding the fabric until it is completely off the needles.

3 Lay the fabric edge between the two large rollers, aligning the raw edge of fabric with the original magic mark. The second magic mark should align with the dominant vertical plaid line.

4 Begin turning the knob and feeding the fabric, as described in the previous exercise (p. 17). Focus your eyes on the second magic mark along the dominant vertical plaid line; do not be concerned with the raw edge at this point.

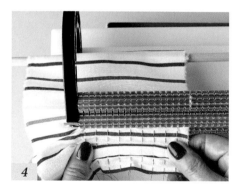

5 Always feed a strip of waxed paper through the pleater to clean and lubricate the needles.

Horizontal and vertical alignment

Plaids can be frustrating to pleat for the beginner, because both horizontal and vertical alignment must be maintained when pleating plaids.

5 Continue pleating the fabric as directed in the previous exercise, keeping your eye on both the vertical and horizontal alignment until the sample has been completed.

Fiber-Etch

Karen Morris

1 first experimented with Fiber-Etch fabric remover in an attempt to simulate the luscious *dévoré* velvets in designer Donna Karan's collection. The word *dévoré* (French for "devoured") aptly describes the burn-out process that produces this look: On velvets with a silk backing and rayon pile, Fiber-Etch eats away the velvet's pile in areas where it's applied, leaving the silk backing intact. If you're busy and have only a limited time to sew, you can create some quick and easy projects by experimenting with Fiber-Etch.

USING FIBER-ETCH

In a nutshell, the burn-out process involves applying a thin layer of Fiber-Etch gel to the wrong side of the fabric, allowing it to dry naturally or with a hair dryer (who can wait?), washing to remove the pile and dried gel, then machine-drying the fabric.

Fluid rayon/silk velvets (usually 82 percent rayon/18 percent silk) work best, because Fiber-Etch will not remove the silk base; it will only remove the rayon pile.

Fiber-Etch is a thick gel that is convenient and easy to work with. I suggest you start by doodling with the gel on samples to see what effects you like and which technique removes the pile cleanly. Directions always tell you to test thoroughly, but this time it's really important. You can end up with uneven results if you don't experiment first. On the charcoal velvet scarf shown on the following page, *dévoré* areas show up in gold because the iridescent fabric was woven with a contrasting pile. On a solid-color velvet, *dévoré* areas will appear as light and sheer sections of the fabric in the same color as the pile.

When working with velvet, instructions for Fiber-Etch suggest using a clothes dryer for the heat stage to

DREAM UP A DESIGN

Now for the fun part. You can create a variety of designs with the gel. Freehand squiggles applied straight from the bottle result in skinny lines that don't show up, but if you spread the bead of gel gently with a clean paintbrush while pressing it into the fabric, the line will have more impact.

Stencils and stickers create, respectively, negative and positive design areas in the pile. Try an office-supply store for press-on labels in a range of sizes and shapes. For the technique described below, for example, I combine labels with stick-on numerals, photo-mounting corners, hole reinforcements, and cut-up decorative seals. I first place the stickers in a pleasing design, then squirt gel in the open spaces, and use a paintbrush to press it in to create a thin, even layer in areas I want to exhaust.

shibori dyeing

You can get great, organic-looking design effects by using techniques borrowed from *shibori* dyeing.

1 Wrap a piece of velvet around a wine bottle (or for a larger piece of fabric, use a long length of PVC pipe). Gather and tie one end of the fabric to the top of the bottle with polyester thread, and tape the other end of the fabric to the bottom of the bottle.

2 Arrange the fabric so there are many small folds, and scrunch it together so the folds are tight, as shown.

avoid crushing the pile.

Out of impatience, I've reverted to the ironing technique described for other fabrics; I figure that since the fabric still needs to be washed, then dried in the dryer, the final drying will fluff up any crushed pile. In fact, a dry iron at a silk/wool setting and a thin press cloth placed on the wrong side of the fabric work well to activate the gel.

After ironing, scratch the pile with a fingernail to see if it's ready to fall out. The flat side of a credit card or a flat, plastic pot scraper is perfect for gently scraping it away. While it's true that rinsing removes the burned-out pile, it also removes the dried gel, so be sure your design has come out cleanly before rinsing.

If the pile isn't completely ready to fall out, iron a little more with the press cloth in place, then scrape again. Be careful not to let the iron get too hot or to hold it too long in one place. Otherwise, the dried gel may burn, especially in spots where it has been thickly applied, and this, in turn, can cause holes in the silk backing.

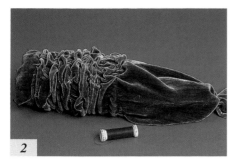

2

While burn-out gel is nontoxic, it makes sense to protect your skin and work surfaces from possible damage. So wear gloves when handling, and cover work areas with a plastic sheet or newspapers. Since pile dust can be irritating when inhaled, wear a mask if you're sensitive. And if gel gets on clothing or skin, wash it off with soap and water.

3 Apply the gel to the tops of all the folds, using a paintbrush to evenly distribute it.

4 After the gel is dry, remove the fabric and iron it.

A second method involves stitching the fabric first.

1 With the machine's longest (6mm) straight stitches, sew a large zigzag design across the fabric. Stop as you reach each edge, as shown.

2 After tying off one end of each "zig," gather and tie off the other end. Repeat for all the stitching.

3 Lay the fabric flat, apply gel to the brush, and paint along the stitching lines, brushing the gel out onto the tops of all the gathers, curves, and folds between rows of stitching.

4 After the gel is dry, remove the stitching and iron it.

The manufacturer also suggests a simple silk-screen method: Stretch a piece of polyester organza or other evenly woven sheer in an embroidery hoop, cut a design in contact paper, and press it on top of the hooped fabric. Place it on the fabric that you are applying the design to, then smooth the gel across the design with a credit-card "squeegee." Press it into the fabric, move the hoop to another section of the fabric, and continue as before.

Try any of these methods on iridescent velvet, which has the backing and pile woven in two different colors. Just imagine the gorgeous effects you could get by burning away part of the pile on a navy/burgundy velvet!

STITCHING FOR *SHIBORI* DYEING

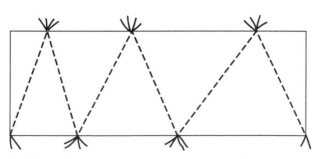

For a stitched *shibori dévoré* scarf, use long, straight machine stitches to sew large, uneven zigzags, ending after each "zig," as shown here.

1

Tassel Magic Kit with Magicord Machine

Cari Clement

T assels and fringe have immeasurable design possibilities, both in home decorating and as wearable accessories. My favorite tool for creating exceptional tassels and fringe is Tassel Magic from Bond America. It comes with instructions, patterns, and all the components needed to make tassels and fringe, including a finial for your first tassel. Some tassels also involve "hard crafts" (such as painting, decoupaging, gluing, etc.) and often can be the perfect outlet for trying out a technique that may interest you.

The Magicord Machine can be used in conjunction with Tassel Magic to make cording, which is used in bullion tassels. This versatile tool is a small, circular knitting machine, which creates knitted cording from thin yarns or threads simply by turning a handle—a contemporary version of the spool knitter. The cording can be very thin (if you use a double strand of sewing thread) or quite thick (if you use baby yarn or yarn of similar thickness); both can be stitched onto fabric using the cording or embroidery foot of your sewing machine. In addition to the machine, the kit comes with a ball of practice yarn, an instruction/pattern book, and an instructional video.

USING THE TASSEL MAGIC KIT

The Tassel Magic kit makes two basic types of fringe: bullion and cut-skirt. Cut-skirt is the most widely recognized type of fringe, in which single

WRAPPING THE YARN

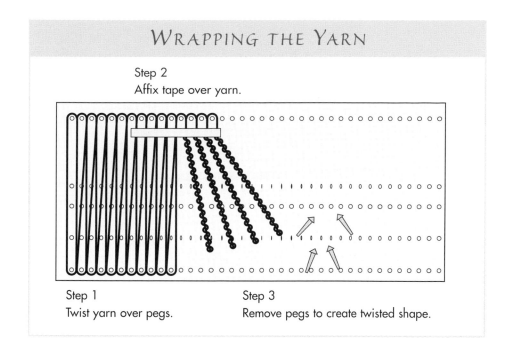

Step 2
Affix tape over yarn.

Step 1
Twist yarn over pegs.

Step 3
Remove pegs to create twisted shape.

strands of thread hang down and are cut at the bottom. Bullion fringe contains one or more strands of yarn that are twisted, then allowed to double back on themselves, creating a rich-looking, rope-like fringe. Bullion is becoming very popular, and the instructions here focus on making bullion tassels.

The Tassel Magic kit contains a board with evenly spaced peg holes both across and down the board. The pegs, included in the kit, secure the yarn, thread, or cord. After positioning the pegs on the board for the desired length of fringe or tassel skirt, simply wrap the yarn around the pegs from top to bottom, and secure the top of the fringe or tassel skirt to the top of the board with tape (also provided in the kit). By removing the lower pegs one by one, elegant, professional-looking fringe is formed.

The most unique part of the Tassel Magic kit is the spinning spool, which is used to twist the yarn for making bullion fringe. It is a wood spool with a dowel in the center, which serves as

the spinner; the spool holds the yarn after it has been twisted. A specially designed spool clip secures the twisted yarn on the spool while more yarn is being twisted. The spool serves the same function as the Magicord Machine but is used specifically for tassel-making.

Choosing material for the tassel parts

There are four main parts to a tassel: the skirt, the ruff, the finial, and the hanging cord (see p. 24).

- For the skirt of a tassel, test the drape of the yarn or fiber you want to use. If the yarn lacks drape but is a color you truly want to use, combine it with a yarn that does have drape, such as rayon thread or floss. The second yarn or thread can even make the resulting tassel skirt more interesting, by adding depth to the overall color. You can also use embroidery floss (cotton, rayon, metallic, or silk), sewing threads,

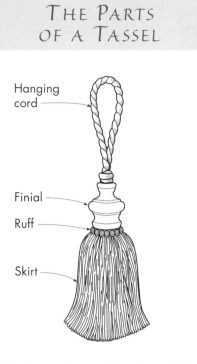

Hanging cord

Finial

Ruff

Skirt

Each part of a tassel can be embellished on its own. The ruff is a decorative device that covers up the joins, and it isn't always included.

decorative serger threads, wool embroidery yarn, or rayon crochet cotton and cording; I've even unraveled old sweaters to use in tassels.

- The **ruff** can be both functional as well as decorative. Although it is usually made from the same or similar materials used for the tassel skirt, try using a string of beads, suede strips, chenille stems, thick chenille yarn, or even a "scrunchie" for the ruff. I found that a decorative candle ring (that slides over a standard candlestick) makes a very dramatic ruff.

- For the **finial**, you can use a wooden decorative top, like the one provided in the Tassel Magic kit. You could also use ordinary items found around the house, such as carpet protectors or caps

from spice containers and roll-on deodorants.

- A **hanging cord** is required to bring the components of the skirt and finial together. This cord can be as decorative as you wish. It is usually made from at least one of the yarns or threads used in the skirt.

I tend to be a pack rat, saving my leftover yarn from other projects and hunting around the house for tassel parts. From a leftover ball of yarn, three skeins of embroidery floss, a package of four chair protectors, and a bit of your time, you can make nearly $100 worth of finished tassels—and custom ones at that!

MULTICOLORED-TASSEL PATTERN

Aside from showing you how to make a tassel, the following instructions will also guide you on how to work with rayon threads. Although rayon is one of the best fibers for color absorption, it can be a bit difficult to work with, due to its slippery nature. Fortunately,

once the thread has been corded, it's much more cooperative.

Two spools of 250-yd./225m rayon thread will be more than enough for a 3-in. bullion tassel. If you'd like a thicker cord, you can use three strands of thread together. For variety, try mixing colors for a tweed effect, or use metallic threads.

(Note: For more detail, refer to the Tassel Magic and Magicord Machine instructions.)

Materials

Two 250-yd. spools of variegated rayon machine-embroidery thread
4 yd. of sewing thread in matching colors
1 finial with a ¾-in. to 1-in. opening at one end and a ¼-in. hole drilled in the closed end
One 1-in.-dia. wood wheel (available at most craft stores)
1 skein of embroidery floss
Crochet hook (size C)
Spray adhesive
Chainette

1 Knit up the entire two spools of thread into cording, using the Magicord Machine. To provide the weight needed to pull the cord through the tube, use one of the two clip weights that come with the Magicord Machine and maintain some added tension on the threads by sliding them through your hand. As it exits the bottom of the tube, wind the cording into a tight ball, securing it with a rubber band.

2 Position the pegs on the Tassel Magic board across the top and bottom rows (depending on the skirt length you want), inserting pegs in every hole.

3

3 Create the bullion by twisting the cording as you wrap it onto the board, following the instructions in the Tassel Magic kit. Continue wrapping around the pegs, alternating top and bottom until you have worked across the board. Tie the yarn to the farthest top-end peg.

4 Affix the tape (provided in the kit) across the top of the board, approximately ⅛ in. below the top row of pegs. Release the wound cording by removing one peg at a time from the bottom row. The yarn will double back on itself to form a bullion. Remove the bullion from the board by lifting it up and over the top pegs, and set it aside.

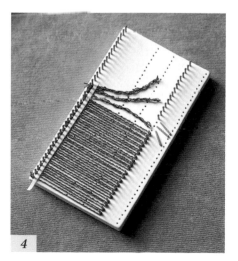

4

5 To decorate the finial, use 4 yd. of the double strand of sewing thread, and knot the two ends together. Follow the instructions in Tassel Magic for making the cording.

6 Apply the spray adhesive (or thick, tacky glue) to the finial. Holding together the cording and one strand of chainette, wrap the lower two-thirds of the finial, ending with the chainette on the top. Affix the ends inside the finial. (If you use tacky glue, work in sections to keep it from drying before you can wind the cord or yarn.)

7 For the ruff, use embroidery floss to make a crocheted chain the circumference of the finial.

8 On the second row, bring up a loop in each of the chain stitches across and keep it on the hook.

9 Apply glue to the flat side of the chain, and affix it to the finial. Let it dry.

10 For the hanging cord, cut 2 yd. of the corded threads used in the skirt and knot the ends together to form a circle.

11 Twist the knitted cording to the desired tightness, and let the cord double back on itself. (Note: You may want to make a few extra twists in the cording since the hanging cord is usually more tightly twisted than the bullion fringe.) Knot the ends together to form a circle.

12 Thread the hanging cord onto the threading wire (provided in the kit), and slide the wood wheel to the knot. To do this, slide the flounce disk (also provided in the kit) over the threading wire and onto the cord, using the knot as a stop. With the open end of the hanging cord at the top, wrap the tassel skirt snugly around the center of the threading wire and tape it to hold.

13 Insert the wire with the tassel skirt into the bottom of the finial, bringing the skirt into the bottom ½ in. of the finial.

14 Flip the finial upside down, and pull through the cording until the flounce disk meets the tassel skirt. Turn the finial right side up, and pull the cording tightly. Your tassel is now complete.

To make cut-skirt tassels, take two or three strands of thread and wind them around the pegs on the board *without* twisting them. Apply the tape just under the top row of pegs, then wind a second layer of fringe over the first layer; apply the tape just above the bottom row of pegs. This ensures that all strands of thread will be caught by either the upper or lower tape. Then remove the lower pegs. Make the tassel according to the kit instructions, and cut the loops at the bottom of the tassel.

One of the most appealing aspects of the Tassel Magic board is its flexibility. You can position the pegs in numerous ways, depending on the types of yarns used and the designs you want to create. Some interesting ways you can alter the pegs include:

- For thick yarn or knitted cording, remove every third peg in the top row to get fringe that is properly spaced for its thickness.

- After making bullion, leave the top loops on the board and reposition the lower pegs to create a second, shorter bullion fringe over the first. This is super for a two-toned or two-textured fringe, such as one layer of chenille and one of rayon.

- For embellishments on tassels, such as added cording or mini-tassels, hang the embellishments or cording over the pegs on the last 2¾ in. of bullion (or the circumference of the base of your finial). After removing the fringe from the pegs, wind the fringe so that the added embellishments will be on the outside of the tassel skirt.

- To add beads, such as for a lampshade trim, twist the yarn onto the spool, then thread the end of the yarn with the beads. Slide them up to the lower peg as you wrap the twisted yarn on the board. When you release the pegs, the beads will remain on the lower edge. Practice on a small section of beaded fringe, testing how the beads hang, to determine the number of beads you will need.

Now, when a pillow is too plain or a window needs a special accent, you can add tassels or fringe for the crowning touch!

Papers for Foundation Piecing

Theresa Robinson

F oundation piecing is the art of joining small, pieced designs together to make a larger, unified design. The basic notion of foundation piecing is the stabilizer, a thin paper used to eliminate the shifting of fabric when it's being sewn. By using a tear-away stabilizer (or what is known as a paper for foundation piecing) under the fabric pieces, it is possible to sew an entire design made up of a number of very small sections.

Thanks to the imagination of quilters, the technique of foundation piecing has come a long way since its beginnings. At first, this technique was used simply to sew small pieces together individually. Quilters began to trace design pieces on squares of stabilizer, then sew these pieces together in stages. This approach led to the technique of sequenced piecing— using an entire design traced on one piece of stabilizing "paper." I like to call it the quilter's version of paint-by-number. This method allows for more precise piecing, exact square sizes, and zero distortion.

USING PAPERS FOR FOUNDATION PIECING

Practice is important to understanding the piecing-by-number technique, but once you master the process it never changes, no matter what quilt design you are sewing. In short, it's a sequential process of sewing pieces of fabric to a stabilizer in numerical order until the design is complete. The pieces create a perfect pattern without precision cutting or sewing, and there is no distortion of the finished square.

The key to success in foundation piecing lies in making sure that the stabilizer pieces are larger than the individual pieces in the design, so that the stabilizer covers the length of the feed teeth. Your sewing machine's feed teeth and presser foot work in unison to move the fabric, but they can sometimes be "confused" by difficult fabrics (for example, if the fabric is too lightweight or too heavy, or if it is cut on the bias). By using a large enough piece of stabilizer, the feed teeth and presser foot are fooled into a false sense of sewing on a smooth and even surface.

For this first exercise, you'll need a few scrap pieces of fabric and a tear-away stabilizer, light to medium weight. The most common brands are Sulky's Tear Easy and America Sews Tear-A-Way. The following steps are based on the simple, sequential, sewing-quilt design pictured here—a log cabin.

1 Cut a square of stabilizer approximately 1 in. larger on each side than the size of the pattern design square. (In this design, for example, cut a 7½-in. square of stabilizer to make the pattern design square shown, which is 5½ in. square.) Place the quilt pattern under the stabilizer. You may want to use a few tiny pieces of tape to hold the quilt pattern in place on the back of the stabilizer.

2 Trace the pattern design and numbers with a fine-point black marker. Make sure you can see your lines from the wrong side of the stabilizer. Wait until the markings are completely dry before starting to sew.

LOG-CABIN QUILT PATTERN

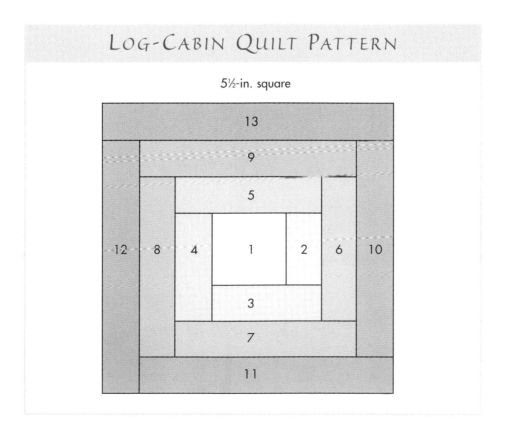

5½-in. square

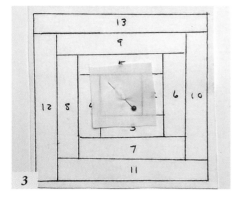

3 Choose a fabric piece for the center square (#1). Cut the fabric so that all sides are at least ¼ in. to ½ in. larger than the traced center square. Place the fabric right side up (facing you) on top of the #1 center square on the stabilizer piece. Use a touch of spray adhesive on the wrong side of the fabric square to hold it in place on the stabilizer.

4 Cut another piece of fabric for section #2 of the quilt design, ¼ in. to ½ in. larger than section #2. Place the #2 piece of fabric over section #2, right side up (do not sew). Make sure there's extra fabric all the way around on the stabilizer. Take your #2 fabric and place it right side together with the #1 fabric, aligning the left edge of the #2 piece with the right edge of the #1 piece. Use a pin to hold it in place.

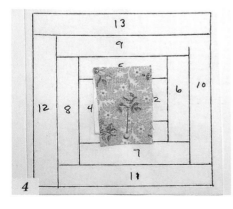

5 Turn the stabilizer piece to the wrong side; the traced lines should be visible from the back. The line between sections #1 and #2 is the stitching line. Set the stitch length at 12 to 14 stitches per inch (1.5–2.0 on most machines today). It is best to start stitching about ¼ in. above the top end of this line to about ¼ in. below the end of this line. (An open-toe presser foot makes it easier to see the line as you sew, so there's no need to backstitch at the start or end of the stitching.)

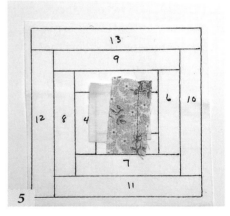

6 Remove the square from the sewing machine, and turn it over to the right side. Pull back the #2 fabric to cover the #2 section, making sure there is extra fabric on all the remaining raw edges. If it still fits well, flip back #2 to the wrong side, and trim the seam to about ¼ in. Now pull back #2 to the right side, and iron or finger-press the seam flat.

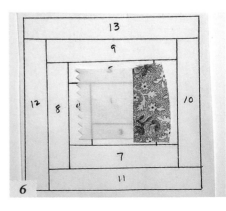

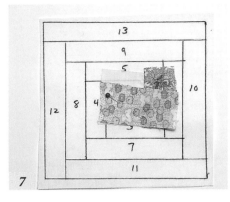

7

7 Cut a piece of fabric larger than section #3. Place this fabric right side up over the top of section #3 for placement. Flip your #3 fabric to lay right side to right side to cover the #1 and #2 edges. Align fabric edges, pin to hold, and turn over to the wrong side.

8 Find the stitching line on the top edge of section #3. Again, start stitching at ¼ in. above the line, and end stitching at ¼ in. below the line. Turn to the right side of the stabilizer, check that there's plenty of fabric around the #3 section, and flip back the fabric to the wrong side to trim the seam. Pull back the fabric to the right side, and press the seam flat.

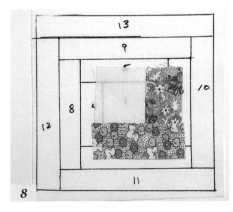

8

9 Repeat steps 3 to 8 to piece together sections #4 through #13.

10 After sewing, trimming, and pressing section #13, turn the stabilizer square to the wrong side. Set your machine on a baste stitch, and baste

on the outside lines of the traced square.

11 On the stabilizer side of the piece, take a pin and carefully score a line, through the stabilizer only, down the middle of each section of design. Pull apart the stabilizer at the scored opening and tear it away from each section. You may need to press the square flat again.

11

When combining several of these squares, it's important that you do not tear away the stabilizer after sewing each individual square. Once you've constructed all the quilt squares for your project, sew them together with the stabilizer still intact. With two squares right side together, match the outside edge lines and pin them together. On the stabilizer side, sew the squares together on the outside line before scoring and tearing away the stabilizers.

Tip

Speed up the process of copying the design by using a special tear-away paper that goes through copying machines. (Using regular tear-away stabilizers in a copying machine can destroy the copier.) Another option is to use this special tear-away paper for printing designs directly from your computer.

Tatool

Mary Libby Neiman

T assels can be used in innumerable ways, both ornamental and functional, in home decor and as clothing accessories. My own "top 10" list of uses includes dressing up a purse, embellishing a jacket, detailing a pillow, and adding tassels to a pull for a ceiling fan or light fixture. A useful tool in making these popular ornaments is the Tatool, a tassel loom that makes creating tassels both simple and enjoyable.

The Tatool is an adjustable steel frame that makes tassels 4 in. to 6 in. long; an extension leg, ordered separately, can make tassels 6 in. to 8 in.

long. There is also a smaller version of the Tatool that aids in the construction of 2½-in. to 4-in. tassels. The device is adjustable, even once a tassel is in progress, so that tension on the warped threads can be increased or eased to properly finish the tassel.

> **Tip**
>
> For "twin" tassels or tassels smaller than 4 in. long, make two at a time by wrapping a neck on both the top and bottom sections of yarn. While it is still wrapped around the frame, cut through the middle of the threads, and you'll have two tassels of the same small size.

USING
THE TATOOL

Before you begin, decide how full you want your tassel to be. Thinner yarns require more lengths than heavier yarns to achieve fullness. Test for the effect you want by bunching groups of yarn; tassels will appear a little fuller when the ends are cut. To determine the amount of yarn you will need for your tassel, multiply the number of yarn lengths by the inches in length of the finished tassel; add 10 percent for take-up and trimming.

1   Begin by placing a temporary yarn or finished hanging cord across the top of the frame. Using masking or transparent tape, tape the cord to the upper corners of the frame. Do not wrap the tape around the frame section; this makes removal of the tape difficult later on.

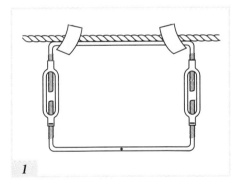

1

2   Adjust the Tatool to the length you want your finished tassel. Stay at least two complete turns away from the smallest setting of the adjusters.

3   Wrap the Tatool as shown. Keep even tension on the thread as you

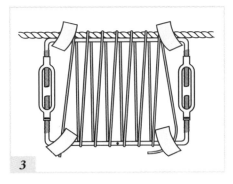

3

wrap. If it is too loose or too tight overall, the device can be adjusted, but uneven tension cannot be corrected.

4   Once all your threads are wound onto the loom and taped down, ease the tension by turning the adjusters one-half turn to the left. Pull the top of the threads together toward the center of the loom to prepare for wrapping the neck. The frame will keep the threads under tension.

5   Choose a smooth, strong yarn for the neck. A medium neck wrapped for ½ in. will require approximately 18 in. to 24 in. of yarn. Tie the neck yarn in a hangman's knot, as shown in 5A. Begin wrapping with the long end (B) at point 1. Wrap

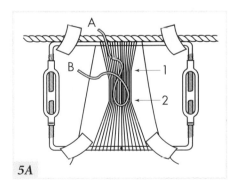

5A

firmly and evenly to point 2 (see 5B). Thread end B through the loop at point 2 (see 5C). Pull end A just until the loop pulls end B under the wrapping. It may help if you keep one thumb on the beginning loop until you have wrapped the top of it three or four times.

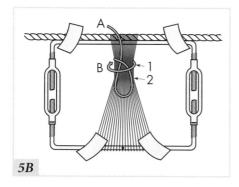

5B

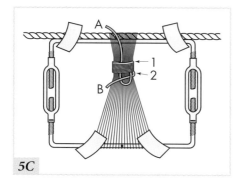

5C

6 Remove the tape from the hanging cord and loosely tie its ends together.

7 Turn the adjusters one turn to the left to shorten the frame. Slide the body of the tassel off the bottom of the frame.

8 Turn the adjusters to the right until the frame comes apart, then slide the top of the tassel off the frame. You may leave the ends looped or cut them with sharp scissors. Depending on the thread and fiber used, you may wish to groom your tassel by shaking and steaming it.

Bullion tassels

Bullion tassels, made of twisted threads or yarns, are made in a similar manner. The only difference is that the yarn must be twisted, using a Spinster or other twisting device, before it is wrapped on the tassel loom. (See p. 36 for a description of the Spinster.)

To calculate the amount of yarn needed to make a bullion tassel, multiply the number of yarn lengths by

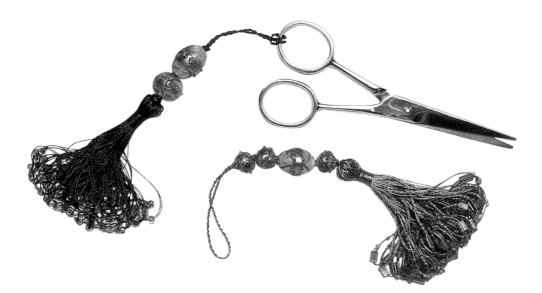

the inches in the length of the finished tassel, double that number, and add 25 percent take-up for twisting.

1 Tape a hanging cord to the top of the Tatool.

2 After your yarn has been twisted, remove one end from the twisting device and hold it firmly between your thumb and forefinger to prevent untwisting. Tape it tightly to the top of the Tatool, as shown.

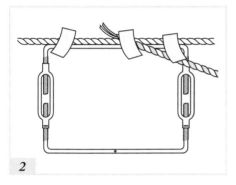

2

3 Wind the length of twisted yarns firmly around the Tatool, keeping the unwound balance on the spool stretched out tightly as you wind. Continue until all the twisted yarn is wound around the Tatool, and finish by taping at the top.

4 Wrap the neck in a hangman's knot as described in step 5 of the basic tassel instructions.

5 Remove the tape from the hanging cord and tie its ends together in a loose overhand knot.

6 Carefully slide one twisted yarn section off the corner to the side of the Tatool. As it exits the bottom of the frame, it will twist into a mini-rope.

7 Use a needle, crochet hook, or your fingers to continue removing each section.

8 Remove the finished tassel as outlined in the basic tassel instructions.

Tip

To make a beaded-fringe bullion tassel, string the beads just before putting the yarn into the twisting device. Then, as you wind the twisted yarn around the Tatool, pull each bead or bead group to the bottom of the Tatool with each turn. Continue the process, as described in the basic tassel instructions, and you'll have a bullion tassel decorated with beads at the bottom of the fringe.

Spinster

Mary Libby Neiman

A popular way to add decorative elements to any garment is to use twisted yarns fashioned into a cord, trim, or rope. By using threads of different but complementary colors, it's easy to jazz up clothing by adding accents using cording.

One of my favorite notions, the Spinster, is a tool designed to help you make custom trim by controlling and manipulating thread, yarn, and wire. It is a device that helps you transform these materials into cord, beaded cord, and bullion trim.

USING THE SPINSTER

For the following instructions, choose the colors of thread or yarn you want to combine to make your cord. Next, determine the length of cord you desire and measure twice that length plus an additional 25 percent to 50 percent for take-up.

The greater the number of elements being twisted and the thicker the individual elements, the higher the percentage you must allow for the

> **Tip**
>
> Cords to be used on an edge of a project must be very firm; you should see and feel a distinct "tooth" that guarantees better protection from pulls and abrasion. Firm cords will require more twists; twist a 1-yd. length first, as a test.

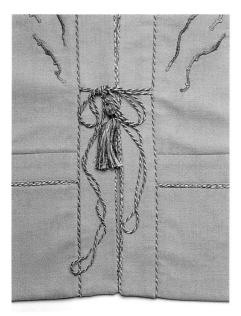

the stationary object so that the threads are taut.

3 Begin twisting the yarn by turning the handle of the Spinster. For a ¼-in. cord that needs a firm finish, turn the Spinster at least 50 times for each yard you have measured; the number and texture of the threads will affect this count. Keep the threads taut as you turn the wheel.

4 When you have finished twisting, place one hand at the midway point of your twisted threads. Insert the hook of the Spinster in the hole on the post of the Quick Grip or in the rubber band on the doorknob. This frees your other hand to assist in finishing. For a long cord, use a weighted chair at the midpoint, wrapping the turned end around the chair back.

5 Continue to keep the cord taut, and pinch the turned end of the cord between your thumb and forefinger. Place your other thumb and forefinger 1 in. away from the turned end;

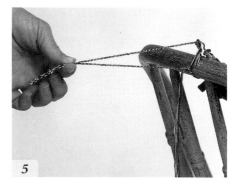

5

bring both strands of twisted yarn together and pinch again. Release the grip on the turned end, allowing your threads to begin twisting back into a cord.

6 Move your thumb and forefinger 4 in. to 6 in. forward, and pinch again. Release the pinch of the other hand, and bring your hands together again,

dimension of the twist. For extremely thick cords, such as those you might use to cord-edge a pillow, you may have to add up to 50 percent or even more. Test to determine your percentage by twisting one yard and measuring the resulting cord.

1 Using a slipknot, attach one end of your group of threads, yarn, or wire to a stationary object, like a doorknob or a Quick Grip. When working with a doorknob, wrap a rubber band over the neck of the knob, tight enough to keep silky threads from slipping. The rubber band will also give you a place to position the hook for finishing.

2 With another slipknot, attach the other end of your threads to the Spinster hook, and hold it away from

2

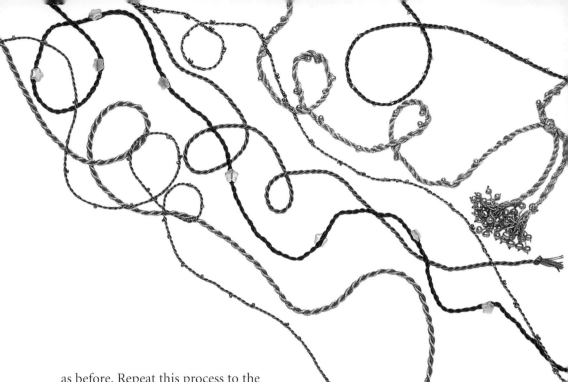

as before. Repeat this process to the end of the cord. When your hands reach the stationary object, remove and release both slipknots, and tie these cut ends together into a firm overhand knot.

Adding beaded elements

It's easy to add beaded elements to your cord before twisting.

1 String all the beads on one thread (or yarn). For tiny beads, use a beading needle.

2 Place the beaded thread beside the other threads to be used in the cord.

3 Prepare the threads with a stationary object and slipknots, as outlined in the basic instructions. Turn the Spinster wheel 5 to 10 times and stop.

4 Put the Spinster on a chair with a weight to keep it in place. Keep it stretched tightly while you walk along the partially twisted rope, and slide the beads to where you want them. To keep this bead placement on the finished cord, restrict your beads to one-half the length of your threads, since this segment will be folded over at its midpoint.

5 Return to the Spinster. Continue to turn the handle and finish as before.

6 You may have to ease the strength of your pinch while smoothing the cord into a twist, as the beads impede easy movement of a tight pinch.

Making rope for custom piping

To make rope for custom piping, use the cording/piping foot on your sewing machine.

1 Center the finished rope on 1¼-in. Seams Great.

2 Stitch along the edge of the rope and press.

3 Fold back Seams Great to form insertion piping.

Stitch rope to Seams Great along one side.

Fold back to create insertion piping.

Making bullion trim

To simulate a bullion embroidery stitch, use two threads. The core thread must be very smooth and strong, and the bullion thread can be either smooth or textured.

1 Cut each thread 1 yd. long. Make a slipknot in each end, and attach one end to a doorknob, the other to the Spinster. Twist together firmly.

2 Remove the knot from the Spinster, and pull the thread ends to release the knot.

3 Hold the core thread with one hand. Pinch and push the other thread along the core toward the doorknob to create the bullion.

Bullion trims can be applied to fabric using a satin stitch or by pulling the cut ends through to the wrong side and securing. You may also choose to make one long, continuous bullion, which can be used as button loops or coiled into decorative elements.

Tip

For extra pizzazz on bullion trim, beads can be threaded and positioned along the smooth core thread. These beads will become part of the finished bullion when the bullion thread is pushed into place.

Cutting and

We've all been told that accurate marking and cutting improve our sewing results. So how do we actually make those accurate marks and cuts? Here, professional sewers discuss their favorite tools and how to use them (sometimes in ways you may not have thought of!). Assess which ones best suit your fabric and the way you work, and improve your sewing in the process.

A pair of scissors and a seam ripper are two of the basics in every sewing kit, but there may be some options you haven't considered. We'll discuss some favorites that have more uses than you think, including the tried-and-true pinking shears. And for when things don't go quite as planned, having the best tools on hand can make all the difference.

Let's not forget the amazing range of marking tools available for the sewer. If you've been marking for years with that same little lump of chalk, look into these methods and tools. You'll be astonished to discover that what was once a tiresome task can become downright enjoyable.

Marking
TOOLS

Pinking Shears

Sue Hausmann

O ne of my favorite notions is a pair of pinking shears. With their saw-toothed blades, these shears allow you to make zigzag cuts in fabric, which help keep the edges from unraveling.

There are many brands and types of pinking shears. I prefer the lightweight, plastic-handled ones because they usually cut synthetic fibers better than the heavier models. Take scraps of fabrics to the store and "try before you buy"; keep in mind that you usually will be cutting two to three layers at a time. The pinking shears should cut cleanly without "chewing" the fabric.

All scissors and shears get dull in time, so be prepared to have them sharpened or replaced as needed. Synthetic fabrics and blends will dull them more quickly than natural fibers. I find it is better to replace my pinking shears every year or two than to have them sharpened; the only way to sharpen them is to send them to the manufacturer, which can be more trouble than it's worth.

USING PINKING SHEARS

I often use pinking shears to save time when a pattern calls for trimming seam allowances. Pinking all layers together creates the same effect as grading—getting rid of the bulk. Pinking shears can also be used to clip curves and to trim edges that would otherwise press through to the right side of the garment.

A pinking rotary cutter can be used for many of the same trimming techniques as pinking shears. I find the rotary cutter easier to use on straight edges, while shears are better with curved seams. The shears and rotary cutter are often interchangeable; try both to see which you like best.

Cutting out fusible interfacings

This technique uses both the pinking shears and the pinking rotary cutter (the latter used with a rotary cutting board).

1 Pin the pattern pieces inside the seamline, and slip the pinking shears under the pattern tissue, cutting along the seamline.

2 Use an interfacing you can see through. Lay it on a rotary cutting board with the pattern on top.

3 Fold the seam allowance back and cut along the seamline with the pinking rotary cutter. The points of the pinked edge will be caught in the seam, leaving no bulk in the seam allowance.

Creating a lined bodice or blouse

When creating a bodice or blouse, a separate facing may show through to the right side or shift during wearing. For an easy professional finish for necklines and for armholes on sleeveless garments, line the bodice or blouse using this technique.

1 Cut one bodice from the fashion fabric and one from the lining. (If there is a back zipper, put it into the bodice as directed. The lining will be sewn to the zipper later.)

2 Stitch the shoulder seams in the bodice and in the lining.

3 Place the bodice and the lining right sides together, and stitch the neckline seam. Trim with pinking shears.

4 Turn the garment right side out, and press the neck edge. Understitch or topstitch as desired.

5 For a bodice with sleeves: Stitch the side seams and then stitch the bodice to the lining at each armhole. Sew in the sleeve, and finish the sleeve seam allowances together.

6 For a sleeveless bodice: After sewing the neckline seam and pressing the neck edge, trim the lining ⅛ in. along the armhole edges.

7 Leave the bodice right side out. Work inside to pin and sew the armholes of the bodice to the lining, right sides together, beginning at the front of one underarm. Sew as far as you can into the shoulder area.

8 When the area is too narrow to continue, remove the garment from the machine and begin sewing at the back of the armhole. This should allow you to stitch all the way around.

9 Trim with pinking shears and press.

10 Sew the side seams of the bodice and lining beginning at the bottom of the bodice—matching underarm seams—and sewing to the bottom of the lining. (I prefer this method to the one that joins the front to the back at the shoulder seams.)

11 If there is a back zipper: Working from the bottom of the bodice, place the lining right sides together with the bodice zipper seam, and stitch or press the seam. Press the lining seam allowance to the wrong side and hand-stitch the lining along the zipper.

A FLEECE SHIRT-JACKET

A great "pinked" project is to create a cuddly shirt-jacket made of fleece, just like those you see in ready-to-wear. Last Christmas I made color-blocked, pinked fleece shirt-jackets for all my

granddaughters. Mixing and matching the bright colors of fleece makes the jackets very attractive—and fun to make.

Materials

Shirt pattern (a basic shirt with a collar and long sleeves with cuffs, cut one size larger than normal)
Fleece fabric (purchase the yardage according to the pattern)
Buttons (according to the pattern)
Sewing thread in a matching color
Pinking shears, or a pinking rotary cutter and cutting mat
Stabilizer
Optional embroidery:
 • Pattern: Husqvarna Viking Collection Card/Disk 8, design 21
 • Sulky 40-wt. rayon embroidery thread

1 Use the main pattern pieces of your selected shirt pattern: front, back, sleeve, collar, and pocket. Eliminate the facing pieces.

2 Cut the fronts, back, sleeves, collar, and pockets with pinking shears. Cut the front edges, collar, and pockets on the seamline and the hem edge of the body and the sleeve on the hemline. The pinked edge will be the finished edge of the front, hems, collar, and pockets.

3 Sew the shoulder, side, and sleeve seams right sides together with a traditional straight stitch on a serger. To keep the shoulder from stretching out, tape the shoulder seam by sewing over a length of clear elastic (do not stretch).

4 For collar and pockets, overlay the pinked edges on the garment, and topstitch. I like to topstitch with a 4.0 or 6.0 twin needle. (If you are having trouble with skipped stitches, use a size 90 stretch twin needle with the blue top.) I use a coverstitch on my Huskylock serger. The coverstitch keeps the seamline from stretching while hanging and wearing. Topstitch the pockets in place. Overlay the collar at the neck edge, and topstitch.

5 Place a cut-away stabilizer under buttons and buttonholes before sewing, to keep them from pulling out and stretching.

Tip

Pink the tape of piping, specialty laces, or picot edge trims before sewing them into a seam. The pinked edge of the tape will curve easily and will not press through as a ridge on the right side.

Clo-Chalk Marker

Clotilde

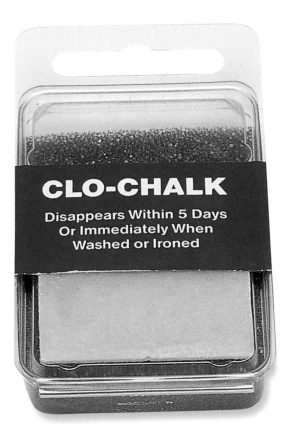

This white disappearing marker looks like standard tailor's chalk. However, with Clo-Chalk, the marks will fade away within three to four days, due to the humidity in the air. If you don't want to wait, you can remove the marks instantly with a shot of steam or a damp cloth. Clo-Chalk does not leave a greasy residue, and it can be used safely on cloth of any color and on delicate fabrics, even silk. To keep the chalk edges sharp, a handy sharpener is included in the package.

Tip

Instead of sharpening Clo-Chalk, designer Kenneth King crushes it with a mortar and pestle, then pours the powder into an empty Chaco-Liner container. It's then ready for instant use.

Clo-Chalk marks clearly visible lines that disappear completely, even on delicate fabrics.

Hera Marker

Linda Lee

W hen a tailor tack is too large and damaging to use on delicate fabrics such as silks and chiffons, I prefer to use a Hera Marker. This is one of the better marking tools simply because no residue is left behind on colored fabric. This tool, made out of bone or plastic, is shaped like a cheese spreader and has one moderately sharp edge, while a curved handle serves as a good, flexible grip.

USING THE HERA MARKER

Drawing a line or making an X using this tool makes a crease in the fabric. The thickness of the tool allows a good deal of pressure to be applied when needed, so that, even on heavy fabrics, the markings are easy to distinguish. On many materials, the marks can be seen even from the underside of the fabric.

No color or residue is transferred to the cloth, and the indentation will remain through the duration of construction. Then, when the project is complete, the markings are impossible to see.

Without leaving a colored mark, the imprint of the Hera Marker is easily distinguished, particularly on heavy fabrics.

Chakoner

Linda Lee

The handiest tool that I keep on my work surface is a Chakoner, and I usually have more than one around. Although I normally use the white Chakoner for marking fabric, it is also available in pink, blue, and yellow. Beware of using the blue and the pink on some fabrics, however; I have found that the chalk may not always disappear.

USING THE CHAKONER

This heart-shaped utensil has a little metal wheel at one end, a removable plastic brush at the other end, and is filled with fine powdered chalk. The chalk is dispensed from the rotating wheel located at the bottom of the container, and the brush easily removes the chalk from the fabric (although the markings usually disappear during construction as well). The line is always consistent in width, and your hands stay clean.

I typically use the Chakoner in tandem with a clear ruler to mark straight lines for cutting or stitching. I also use it to mark tagboard templates for curved or odd shapes and for drawing around the template edges.

Another variation of the same tool is Clover's Chaco-Liner. It also makes beautiful, clear lines, but the shape of the case is different from the Chakoner. It is the size of a lipstick tube, with a screw end and a plastic cover. It also has replacement powder and is available in the same four colors as the Chakoner. Deciding which one to buy depends on the shape that feels comfortable in your hand.

The rotating wheel of a Chakoner makes it easy to get right up against a ruler, for smooth, clear, and accurate marks.

Clover Seam Ripper

Linda Lee

A seam ripper, unfortunately, is one of my best friends. I use it often, so I want it to be ultrasharp and extrafine—but not a dagger! The Clover Seam Ripper meets all of these qualifications.

The bold plastic handle is easy to hold, and a band of ribbed black rubber around one end of the handle keeps my hand from slipping and losing its grip. The metal point and cutter are razor sharp; the point is able to reach the smallest stitches, and the almost-hidden cutter slips easily into a tricky place. The tiny red knob on the smaller point probably has a function, too, but mostly it just makes me smile.

USING THE CLOVER SEAM RIPPER

Ripping can be hazardous if not done properly. I use the longest prong of the ripper to slip under a stitch that is lying on top of the fabric, and cut it.

Then I spread the two pieces of fabric apart and begin to cut the stitches as they spread. Try to cut no more than one or two stitches at a time, and absolutely never run the ripper down the center of the stitch line to cut an entire seam in one motion, or you might damage the fabric. Patience prevails when ripping seams.

Just as I replace my pins and needles on a regular basis, I also buy a new ripper every once in a while. At under $4, it's a bargain.

The long prong of the Clover Seam Ripper slips neatly under stitches, cutting through them without damaging the fabric.

Rainbow Braid

Linda Lee

O
ne of the secrets to precision sewing is good markings. I always mark clearly before removing cut fabric from my cutting table, so that I don't have to hunt for the identifying symbols later. In addition to marking dots, triangles, and squares before sewing, I also mark pressing and stitching lines during the sewing process.

One of my favorite marking tools is an embroidery floss for tailor tacks called Rainbow Braid. It's a wonderful package of braided, 100 percent polyester embroidery floss. This multicolored braid looks like a crocheted ribbon, but it consists of 348 strands of 27-in. precut usable floss in 29 colors. With so many colors from which to choose, you can always find, in one handy place, an embroidery floss that will work with your fabric.

USING RAINBOW BRAID

To use Rainbow Braid, simply pull out one 8-ply piece of floss from the woven braid in the color of your choice, then thread a sharp needle with a fairly large eye. For marking dots, slash lines, corners, and pivot points, as well as triangles and squares (to identify darts), make only one stitch instead of the classic two-step tailor tack, leaving about 1-in. tails. Then spread the two pieces of fabric apart and snip the floss, so that you have a smaller tack in each piece.

Since embroidery-floss tacks stay in the fabric, you don't have to worry about them falling out before you start the construction process. When you are finished with your project, the multiple strands pull out easily.

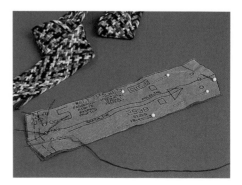

Tailor tacks are a quick and accurate way to transfer pattern markings to your fabric.

Tracing Wheel and Tracing Paper

Susan Khalje

For all of the technical advances that have been made in sewing technology and the streamlining of techniques, some tried-and-true methods are hard to improve upon. Marking with tracing paper and a tracing wheel is one such method; it's accurate, versatile, and relatively quick. Whether you're marking stitching lines, important placement lines, or grain lines, carefully and accurately applied markings are an indispensable part of any successful sewing project.

My favorite tracing wheels are the simple, inexpensive plastic or wood-handled ones, with a single, serrated blade. Avoid spiked patternmaker's tracing wheels, which could damage your fabric; smooth-bladed wheels, which don't grip the fabric very well, thus reducing your accuracy; and wheels designed to partially cover the blade, making it difficult to see exactly where the wheel is hitting the fabric.

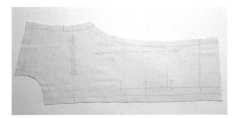

A well-marked garment section will show a number of useful marks, including stitching lines, dart lines, pocket placements, and button and buttonhole placements.

Like the tracing wheel, some types of tracing paper should also be avoided. For example, no-wax tracing paper is covered with powder, which comes off on your hands, the work surface, and anything else the paper touches. Other kinds of tracing paper leave imprints that disappear in time (much like the marks left by the purple disappearing-ink marking pens); apart from leaving a chemical residue on your fabric, your sewing time is limited since the traced marks last only a short time. I like to use waxed dressmaker's carbon, also known as professional transfer paper/carbon paper.

Tracing paper is sold in large sheets of red, blue, yellow, and white. Because of its size, you may want to mount the paper on a large piece of cardboard or cut it into smaller sections. If you store the paper rolled up, the corners of the paper may curl; just tape the corners to your work table or weigh them down.

USING A TRACING WHEEL AND TRACING PAPER

Before doing any tracing, experiment with various colors of carbon paper and figure out how much pressure to exert with the tracing wheel. Use an especially light hand when the tracing paper is new and heavily coated with wax. In some cases, marks may show through onto the right side of the fabric, which means you'll either have to use a less conspicuous color of carbon

> **Tip**
>
> Always mark white fabric with white tracing paper, unless the marks will be hidden in an inner layer. White markings on white or light-colored fabric can be difficult to see, but changing your light source or the color of your work surface can help. The traced marks will be more visible if you move to a darker colored work area or cover your work space with a darker fabric.

paper or a lighter touch. If you're using an underlining in a garment, the tracing lines will go onto the underlining, sparing the fashion fabric from having to be marked. Even so, it's a good idea to check this ahead of time; you may be surprised at what shows through.

Also, check that the tracing wheel doesn't cut the fibers of your fabric. Satin weaves (satin, charmeuse, and satin-backed crepes) and ribbed fabrics (moiré, faille, and taffeta) can be ruined by too much pressure from a tracing wheel. Also, check to see what happens to the marks once they've been ironed. Sometimes they disappear (especially white on black), but sometimes they intensify (yellow on white often does). It may or may not matter, but you need to know.

Finally, with today's multisized patterns, you may have to do a little pattern preparation before you trace. If you want to trace the stitching lines, you'll first have to mark them on the pattern piece. The metal tips of most tape measures are ⅝ in. wide; use one as your guide when marking the stitching lines on the pattern piece.

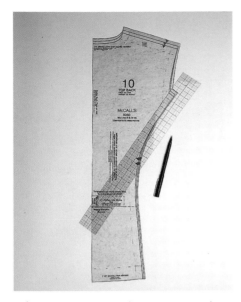

Before tracing, prepare the pattern piece by marking the stitching lines and any other pertinent information.

After all this experimenting, you're ready to trace. You can fold a piece of tracing paper, carbon side out, and sandwich it between two layers of fabric (thus marking the inner sides of the fabric), or you can fold the tracing paper, carbon side in, and enclose two layers of fabric (thus marking the outer sides of the fabric). There is another way to mark, however, which ensures greater accuracy:

1 Place the tracing paper, carbon side up, on the work surface. On top of the tracing paper, lay the fabrics you wish to mark—generally two layers of fabric with a pattern piece securely pinned on top of them.

2 With the tracing wheel, trace what you need to mark—stitching lines, dart lines, hemlines, button and buttonhole placement lines, decorative detail placements, etc. The marks will be applied to the fabric that's touching the carbon, that is, the layer at the bottom. When tracing notches and match points, stay within the seam allowances to lessen the chance of the markings showing through inside the stitching lines. Use an especially gentle hand when marking darts so that the markings don't show through.

3 Before removing the pattern piece, take a quick look to check that you've marked everything. Carefully remove the paper, then immediately reinsert the pins into the fabric so that the two layers are still together.

4 Flip the fabric over to see the marks you've just made. Use those marks as a guide for tracing the second side.

> *Tip*
>
> To prevent the fabric from bunching up in front of the tracing wheel, try rocking the blade of the wheel as you go along. With your free hand, gently hold the fabric taut in front of the tracing wheel.

1

Duckbill Scissors

Barbara Deckert

D uckbill scissors, also known as appliqué scissors, likely got their name from their interesting shape. They are small and have one normal-looking blade and one semi-circular blade, which somewhat resembles a duckbill. The duckbill blade helps you cut more accurately without cutting through the fabric, especially when grading seams.

Both Mundial and Gingher make duckbill scissors, but chrome-plated Ginghers are my favorite. They have a very sharp knife-edge, which can be easily sharpened with a sharpening stone (also by Gingher).

> **Tip**
>
> For grading only a few layers, trim the entire seam allowance by half. Then go back and use the appliqué scissors to grade each of the individual allowances to different widths, to reduce bulk.

USING DUCKBILL SCISSORS

My favorite uses for duckbill scissors include grading seams, clipping seams, opening machine buttonholes, and trimming appliqués. The scissors make all of these procedures both fast and easy.

Grading seams

As you construct a garment, you should grade all the seam allowances that end up enclosed inside the garment and that do not need to be finished; you can trim these seam allowances different widths, from relatively narrow to relatively wide. The purpose of grading is to reduce bulk inside the garment and to make the finished piece thinner and flatter.

The ready-to-wear industry seldom grades seams anymore, but if you look closely at collars, lapels, flaps, cuffs, and the like, you'll often see unattractive ridge lines along the thick and overly pressed seams. Home sewers can do it better, and appliqué scissors make this process fast and easy.

Before you begin grading, determine which of the seam allowances needs to end up the widest. On a typical blouse with a collar, facing, and sewn-in interfacing, the neckline seam allowance has six layers of fabric to grade: the blouse itself, front and back; the under collar; the collar interfacing; the top collar; the facing; and the facing's interfacing. On the finished garment, the blouse seam allowance will lie next to the blouse front and back to give a smooth impression on the garment's right side, so the front and back neckline seam allowances should be the widest of the six layers.

1 Hold the seam allowance that will be trimmed the shortest facing you. In the case of a blouse, the facing's interfacing should be toward you.

2 Use the duckbill-shaped blade to lift the uppermost layer of the seam allowance, and trim it close to the stitching of the neckline seam. For tightly woven fabrics and garments with a small stitch length, trim to ⅛ in. to 1/16 in.; for thicker, more loosely woven fabrics or garments with longer stitches, trim to ¼ in. to ⅛ in.

3 Continue to trim each successive layer of seam allowances a bit wider than the first, so that they are graduated from the narrowest to the widest. Don't measure the widths; just trim by eye. Because this particular seam has many layers, the finished seam allowance may still be ⅜ in. wide.

3

Clipping seams

Duckbill scissors have such sharp points that they are perfect for clipping seams once you've graded them. Nearly all curved seams must be clipped so they will be the right shape when the garment or its pieces are turned right side out.

For example, on a curved collar, such as a Peter Pan collar, the seamline on the wrong side of the collar is convex, while the seam allowance is concave when turned right side out. Clipping the seam allowances causes the collar seam allowance to bend in the opposite direction so it will lie flat and hold the desired shape of the collar. This process is sometimes called "releasing the curve."

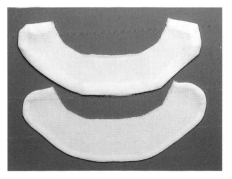

The difference between clipped and graded seams is obvious in these two Peter Pan collars. The one with clipped seams (bottom) holds the curvy shape better and is less bulky to the touch.

To clip a seam, simply snip through the seam allowance at a right angle to the seam, close to the stitching. For tight curves, cut about ¼ in. apart; for gradual curves, you can cut up to 1 in. apart. To determine if you've clipped enough, hold each end of the clipped seam in your hands and gently pull the seam straight. If the ends don't come together in a straight line, cut a few more clips to further release the curve.

In addition to clipping all interior curved seams, you should also clip all other curved, plain seams before finishing the seam allowances, such as a princess seam that follows the curves over the bust.

Opening machine buttonholes

Using the small, sharp blades of appliqué scissors is also the fastest way to open a machine-made buttonhole. Simply fold the buttonhole in half lengthwise and snip between the buttonhole stitches, just at the fold. Then unfold the buttonhole, slip the smaller blade into the snip, and continue to cut the buttonhole open to the bar tacks at the end. This method sounds a bit scary, but it has never failed me.

Trimming appliqués

Duckbill scissors were made for trimming appliqués without nicking the fabric underneath. For reverse appliqués:

1 Remove the topmost layer of appliqué to expose the under layer.

2 After stitching the appliqué in place, carefully pinch a fold in the top layer at the middle of the area to be trimmed. Use your scissors' blade to snip a small hole at the fold.

3 Insert the small blade into the hole to snip to the appliqué stitching.

4 Use the duckbill blade down and the regular blade up to lift and trim the top layer close to the stitching, exposing the contrast underneath.

The wide lower blade keeps you from accidentally cutting into the fabric under layer.

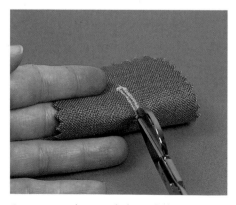

Opening machine-made buttonholes with duckbill scissors makes the task safe and easy.

Sew Clean

Theresa Robinson

W hile many sewing marks are intentional, others are not. Accidents happen. You spill, splash, and drop things, usually on the fabric you are diligently working on or pressing at the time. You can try all the established "fixes" for each kind of stain—white wine, vinegar, salt, cold water, hot water, etc. Or you can reach for Sew Clean, an all-natural fabric spot-and-stain remover.

Sew Clean is a nontoxic, biodegradable citrus extract, which contains no butyl or harsh alkalines. It removes most common stains: ink,

pencil, and crayon marks; lipstick and makeup; fingerprints; blood and grass stains; oil, grease, and rust; stains from coffee and soft drinks; and chewing gum. It also cleans glass, ceramic tile, plastics, painted surfaces, carpet, fiberglass, and more.

The directions are easy. Simply spray the stain, and use a dampened cloth to blot it out. For tiny spots, use a cotton swab dipped in Sew Clean. It's also great as a prewash treatment in the laundry. Sew Clean comes in a 12-oz. plastic bottle with a spray nozzle.

part THREE

Pressing is an important part of the sewing process. Depending on the project you are working on, you may spend more time at the ironing board than you do at the sewing machine. If you don't press seams as you sew, your projects will shout "homemade." So spend the extra time and press as you go.

The proper equipment is essential for getting the best results. If you've spent a lot of money on a fabric, don't ruin it by not using the right pressing tool. All of the items included in this section are readily available to the home sewer and are well worth the money. The uses for each piece of equipment are discussed in detail, as well as the appropriate time to use them.

pressing AIDS

Tailor's Ham

Barbara Deckert

A tailor's ham, similar in shape to a canned ham, is used when pressing to simulate curves and shapes of the body, making it easier to press seams and to shape garments properly.

Firmly stuffed with sawdust or polyurethane, a tailor's ham is covered on one side with canvas, useful for pressing most fabrics, and on the other side with wool, for pressing woolens. There are three types of tailor's hams:

- A **standard tailor's ham** features convex curves that reproduce nearly all the curves on the human body. The wider end of the ham is fairly flat, so it can be set on its wider end to allow garment pieces to be shaped over its narrow end.

- A **dressmaker's ham** is similar to a tailor's ham but is more oval shaped and without a flat end.

- A **contoured tailor's ham** features concave as well as convex curves. (Note: The plastic ham holder shown in the photo is no longer available.)

I prefer the standard tailor's ham, because I can hold the ham in one hand, drape the garment over the ham with the other hand, and then pick up my iron to steam or press the garment.

USING A TAILOR'S HAM

A ham is used to press all curved seams such as darts, collars, cuffs, yokes, pockets, and flaps that lie over curved areas of the body. It helps shape the fabric to fit the body's curves and usually holds that shape for the lifetime of the garment.

Pressing plain, curved seams

1 Clip the seam allowances as little as needed to release the curves, then finish the edges to prevent fraying.

2 With the seam allowances still together, press the seam allowances flat using your ironing board. This shrinks the stitches into the fabric and makes the seam smoother and stronger; this process is often called "setting the seam" or "setting the stitches."

3 Lay the seam right side down over the part of the ham that looks most like the appropriate body curve. Hold the ham at either end or on its side, and press the seam open.

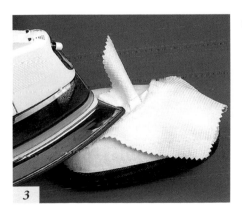

Pressing darts

Darts accommodate our curves, so they need to be pressed over the curved surface of a ham.

1 First, press the dart flat to reduce bulk and to set the stitches. Be careful to press only the dart, not the rest of the garment.

2 Lay the garment right side down on the ham. Press the dart away from the center of the garment to give it a sharp crease, then press the dart back toward the center of the garment.

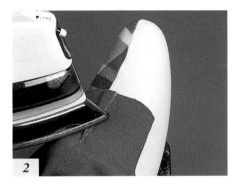

3 Use your fingers to gently stretch the fabric on both sides of the dart stitching line; pay particular attention to the dart tip to avoid creating a dimple.

Tip

Some darts, such as double-pointed waist darts, should be clipped once in the center before pressing, to release their curves.

4 Next, check the dart on the right side of the garment. If necessary, top-press very lightly over the ham with a press cloth, or use steam and your fingers to gently stretch out any dimple at the dart tip. To avoid a ridge line, be careful not to overpress at the dart fold.

Shaping collars, lapels, cuffs, flaps, and other garment components

1 Once the garment piece has been constructed and is ready to attach to the body of the garment, find the place on your ham that looks most like the size of the body part that the finished component will cover. On a tailored jacket collar, for example, choose the wide end, the middle, or the narrow end of the tailor's ham that most closely resembles your neck size.

2 Fold the collar at the roll line, as it will be worn.

3 Wrap the collar around the ham, at about the same angle that it will be on the finished garment, and pin it in place, right into the ham.

4 Without touching the fabric, use your iron to steam the roll line.

5 Allow the fabric to cool and dry thoroughly before removing the collar from the ham.

You can also use a ham to give some shape to flat collars, cuffs, and flaps, by top-pressing these pieces with a press cloth over the ham.

Sleeve Roll

Barbara Deckert

*U*nlike a sleeve board, which has flat pressing surfaces for ironing wrinkles out of finished sleeves, a sleeve roll is shaped like a long cylinder. The curved pressing edge and narrow shape make pressing open sleeve seams and other small seams a snap.

USING A SLEEVE ROLL

In addition to pressing open sleeve seams, sleeve rolls are perfect for pressing open seams on fragile fabrics that tend to show seam-finish impressions, such as satins. Forget those prissy strips of brown paper under the seam allowances; just place the seam over the length of the roll and gently press the seam open. The finished edges of the seam allowances will drop down over the high point of the sleeve roll's curve. There's virtually little or no contact with the iron as you press and, as a result, no imprint.

Tip

For stiff and very fragile fabrics, use only the very tip of the iron to open the seam.

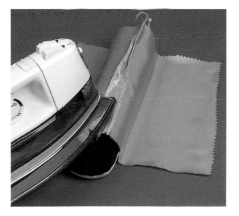

When you don't want seam allowances to leave an impression, press them open on a sleeve roll.

Point Presser

Barbara Deckert

A point presser is an anvil-shaped tool made of hardwood that allows you to make a sharp press on straight seams, facings, and points. One brand, called a Tailor Board, is more useful than a standard point presser because its extra curves and angles reproduce nearly every garment and body curve imaginable, providing more options than a ham for accurate pressing. It can be placed in 12 versatile positions, enabling you to arrange the best surface for pressing.

The Tailor Board is useful on princess and other curved seams, as well as inside small garment pieces to press open seam allowances or to press them to one side. It's also useful for pressing small, hard-to-reach areas such as sleeve caps.

USING A POINT PRESSER

You can use a point presser for seams with curves tighter than a ham can easily accommodate (for example, a small size with a large bust). To press a tight princess seam:

1 After sewing, clip and finish the seam. Find the curve on the Tailor Board that most closely matches the bust curve; usually, this will be the long, outward curve.

2 Lay the seam wrong side up, and use only the tip of the iron to press open the seam allowances.

3 If needed, flip the piece over and use steam and a few gentle pats with your fingers to set the seam.

4 Leave the seam on the board until the piece is completely cool and dry.

1

Press Cloth
and Iron Shoe

Barbara Deckert

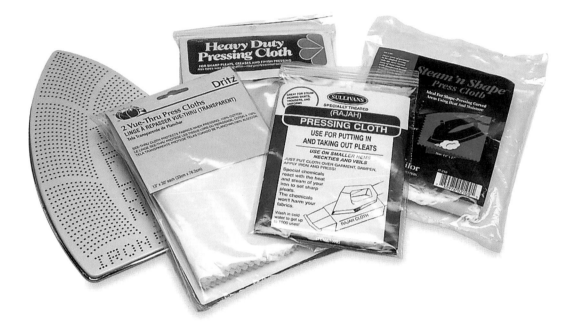

P ress cloths and iron shoes
protect fabrics from shine,
scorch, and press marks. I always use
them when pressing the right sides of
fabrics, particularly woolens,
worsteds, and silks, as well as fragile
fabrics that mar easily, like satins.

TYPES OF PRESS CLOTHS

You can select from a variety of press
cloths; your choice depends on the
type of fabric you're pressing.

- Plain press cloths are widely
  available and can be used for
  most types of fabrics. You can
  also use a plain piece of cotton
  muslin as a press cloth.

- Teflon-coated press cloths prevent
  starch, resins from fusibles, and
  other chemicals in fabrics from
  sticking to your fabric, the press
  cloth, and your iron. Teflon- or
  metallic-coated ironing board
  covers are treated cloths that
  could reflect heat, so you may
  need to use a lower-than-
  recommended iron setting to
  avoid melting some fabrics—
  while fusing, for example.

- Artificial chamois cloths look like
  felt and hold a tremendous
  amount of moisture, which dis-
  perses slowly as you press. As a
  result, these cloths are especially
  helpful when working with
  woolens or with wrinkly and

The heat and steam of an iron releases chemicals from the Rajah Press Cloth that set sharp, professional creases and pleats without harming the fabric.

trousers, pleats, and uniforms made out of a 50/50 blend of polyester and cotton. These chemicals are harmless to fabrics, and the cloth works for up to a thousand uses.

IRON SHOES

Iron shoes attach to your iron and are heat proof. Not only do they protect your fabric, they also protect your iron from scratches, resin, and starch buildup. These shoes make pressing faster, as well, since you do not have to reposition a press cloth as you iron. The only drawback to these shoes is that sometimes it is difficult to get a sharp press with the tip of the iron. The tip of the shoe, which is larger than the iron's soleplate, doesn't heat up as well as the tip of the iron itself.

One brand, Iron-Safe, has a metal, soleplate-shaped frame that holds a laminated, perforated Teflon material; springs hold the shoe on your iron, and steam easily permeates the perforations. It fits most irons except Rowenta. Another brand, the Magic Slipper, is a Teflon "shoe" perforated with holes that allow the steam to go through.

hard-to-press fabrics, such as linens. For pressing, wet the chamois and then squeeze as much liquid out of the cloth as possible, so your work doesn't become too wet. Chamois cloths—with brand names such as Pressit Steam Pressing Cloth and Steam and Shape—are available from auto-supply stores and from shops that sell household items.

- Special-use press cloths, such as the Rajah Press Cloth, are impregnated with chemicals that help set permanent creases in

Tip

Always test-press using fabric scraps, to be sure you won't ruin your fabric.

Needle Board

Barbara Deckert

eedle boards are useful for pressing all fabrics with pile, such as velvet and velveteen, corduroy, chenille, fleece, and terry cloth. The needles support the area being pressed, right side down, so that the piling does not crush. As a result, steam or gentle pressing on the wrong side ensures that the fabric emerges without any damage.

TYPES OF NEEDLE BOARDS

There are two types of needle boards:

- **Steel needle board.** This old-fashioned standby, made by Dritz, consists of a laminated canvas board that has thousands of tiny, sharp needles. (It looks like a bed of nails for a Barbie doll.) The steel needles point straight up and are very closely spaced, so they completely support the most fragile of piles. The base is slightly flexible, so you can press gently curved areas. My own steel needle board has served me faithfully for 25 years.

- **Industrial Needle Board.** This Velcro-like board has bristles that are shorter than the nails on a steel needle board. I like to use it for fairly sturdy, shorter pile fabrics such as velveteen, corduroy, or chenille. One brand I like is the June Tailor Velvaboard. About the size of a dishtowel, this needle board has a finely perforated, flexible base, and its bristles are made of plastic. Its large size is great for steaming and pressing big areas or for opening long seams without frequent repositioning.

Press velvet, corduroy, and embroidered fabric using an Industrial Needle Board, which won't flatten the pile or nap of the fabric.

Spray Water Bottle

Barbara Deckert

An ordinary utility sprayer is a handy tool to have in your sewing room. Widely available in stores selling household goods, a spray water bottle offers a more genteel alternative to the old "spit and scratch" method.

USING A SPRAY WATER BOTTLE

A little cool water spray is terrific for removing fabric markings. Simply spray a fine mist over the water-soluble marks for instant results.

Water is also helpful in getting out irritating creases, tenacious wrinkles, and annoying pinholes. If your fabric does not water spot, a quick spray and a press will eliminate nearly all wrinkles and stubborn creases (like the foldline down the middle of a bolt of fabric). Do a quick fabric test, just to be sure. If your fabric does water spot, try using a muslin press cloth over the area; lightly spray the press cloth only, and then press through the cloth. In the case of pinholes caused by ripping out a seam, spray the pinholes, rub them gently with your fingertips, and press.

No-Stick Sheet

Clotilde

O ne of my favorite notions has been used for years not only by sewers but also by fast-food restaurants and the food-processing industry. It's the No-Stick Sheet and its partner, the See-Thru No-Stick Sheet, which were introduced over 10 years ago.

Both sheets are made of fiberglass impregnated with Teflon, the forerunner of the No-Stick Sheet. Teflon was first introduced to the appliqué world to keep fusible web from sticking to the soleplate of the iron, which previously required tedious clean-up. The No-Stick Sheet is an improved version of Teflon; it is tough, stays flat, and withstands heat up to 600°F. It can also be cut with scissors but won't tear accidentally.

The See-Thru No-Stick Sheet is often called an "appliqué sheet," because you can see the appliqué underneath. The sheet also "breathes," allowing moisture to go through it. Simply place the appliqué and the fusible web between two layers of the See-Thru No-Stick Sheet to fuse the appliqué and the web together. Now they are fused without leaving any residue on the iron or the board.

These sheets are a lifesaver for the home sewer, crafter, or cook because nothing sticks to them. Because the sheet resists chemicals, it doubles as a protective sheet for any counter or work surface. In the kitchen, its 18-in. by 20-in. size is perfect to line a baking pan or cookie sheet, and it can even be used to roll out pie dough. There are virtually dozens of uses for these strong No-Stick Sheets.

The No-Stick Sheet protects your iron from fusible interfacings.

Stabilizing

and

S tabilizers are what keep a garment or project in shape through all the wear and tear of manufacture and everyday use. They prevent wrinkles and puckers, and add stiffness when the fabric is too floppy. Often, when a project is less successful than you'd hoped, it's because the wrong stabilizer (or no stabilizer) was used. There are a huge variety of stabilizers available, from the traditional ones that couturiers have been using for years to new products that add speed and convenience along with structure.

Each of these stabilizers has a wide range of applications, some of which may improve the way your project looks and wears, in addition to giving it a more professional appearance. For example, if you're sewing a T-shirt, clear elastic will make the shoulder seams more durable. Or, if you're working on something more formal and want to add a little flare, try using horsehair for maximum effect. One of these products may be just right for your current needs or a valuable option for future reference.

Structuring Aids

Tear-Away Stabilizer

Carol Ahles

I have avoided many sewing problems simply by using tear-away stabilizers. Not only do stabilizers keep garments in shape once they are complete, but they also make the construction process go more smoothly. Stabilizers help to "tame" the fabric—keeping it steady and in place as you sew and eliminating any shifting or puckering that could ruin your stitches. For example, wide stitches can cause a fabric to tunnel, if you don't stabilize the fabric. Spray starching and pressing help somewhat—and a hoop may be used when appropriate—but a light tear-away stabilizer placed under buttonholes,

satin stitching, appliquéing, and most decorative stitching usually does the trick.

I prefer lightweight stabilizers for most applications, especially under light- to medium-weight fabrics. If you need more stability (for example, on hooped computerized machine embroidery), you can use multiple layers of stabilizer. You could also opt for a heavier stabilizer, but it can sometimes distort delicate fabrics or the stitching when it is torn away.

Fortunately, lightweight tear-away stabilizers are readily available. Names to look for are Tear-Easy from Sulky, Jiffy Tear-Away from Staple Sewing

Aids Corporation, Easy Tear from Graphic Impressions, Stitch & Ditch from Thread Pro, No Whiskers from Clotilde, and Armo Tear-Away from HTC. Many of these brands are available by mail order through sewing catalogs, as well as from sewing-machine dealers and fabric shops.

USING A TEAR-AWAY STABILIZER

Before starting your project, do a little test-stitching first. Use the fabric, needle, thread, and stabilizer you plan to use on the project. It's important that your test-stitching be on the same grain as it will be in your project. Lengthwise stitching (parallel to the selvage) tends to pucker and tunnel more—and thus needs more stabilizing—than crossgrain stitching.

Put the tear-away stabilizer under the fabric before stitching. In some cases, it can be easily held in place; if not, pin through the fabric and stabilizer from the right side to keep it from shifting, and remove the pins as you stitch near them. Another option is to adhere the stabilizer in place with a temporary spray adhesive. Lightly spray the stabilizer over a press cloth or paper, then apply it to the underside of the fabric.

When you must start stitching at the very edge or corner of the fabric, often it is not possible to have the fabric securely under the presser foot and over both feed dogs at the same time. In this case, put the edge of the fabric over the corner of a small piece of tear-away stabilizer. This gives the sewing-machine feed dogs something to grab onto for help in feeding the fabric, allowing the fabric to move smoothly from the very beginning. Afterward, gently tear away the bit

Pinning the edge of the fabric together with a small piece of tear-away stabilizer helps your sewing machine make smooth stitching right from the fabric's edge.

of stabilizer that is caught in the stitching.

To keep delicate stitching and fabric from being distorted when tearing away the stabilizer, pinch the stitching between your thumb and index finger and tear the stabilizer up to your thumbnail. If you're using multiple layers of stabilizer, tear away one layer at a time to avoid any damage to the fabric.

To avoid disturbing any delicate stitching, gently tear away the stabilizer a small section at a time.

> **Tip**
> Some stabilizers tear more easily in one direction than another. Check this before stitching to ensure easy removal of the stabilizer, as well as to reduce distortion and "whiskers."

Cut-Away Stabilizer

Pat Welch

A cut-away stabilizer is a non-woven, permanent stabilizer. Once it's sewn in, it stays in; the only way to remove it, once it's in the garment, is to cut it out. Of the four types of stabilizers—tear-away, cut-away, wash-away, and heat-away—cut-aways are the only permanent ones. They not only provide support while stitching, they also help keep the garment together while washing and wearing. Cut-aways are recommended for all knits, any unstable

fabric, and heavily embroidered garments. They are ideal for delicate fabrics as well, because cut-aways help prevent sagging and pulling.

The two types of cut-away stabilizers are Cut-Away Soft 'n Sheer and Cut-Away Plus. Cut-Away Soft 'n Sheer is a sheer, supple, nonwoven nylon. It feels like silk next to the skin and is great for babies and people with sensitive skin. Since it doesn't leave a shadow effect like other stabilizers, Soft 'n Sheer works well with sheer fabrics as well as T-shirts, single knits, panne velvets, open weaves (such as hand wovens), Lycra, velours, and double knits. Cut-Away Plus, a thicker version of the cut-away stabilizer, is ideal for outerwear and heavier knits (such as sweatshirts), and it won't ravel.

USING A CUT-AWAY STABILIZER

To use a cut-away stabilizer, hoop it together with your fabric. For added support, you may want to use a combination of Soft 'n Sheer with a tear-away stabilizer, one layer of Cut-Away Plus, or two to three layers of Soft 'n Sheer. Choose your needle depending on the kind of fabric you have. With knits and fine silks, use a ballpoint needle; with woven fabrics, choose an embroidery needle.

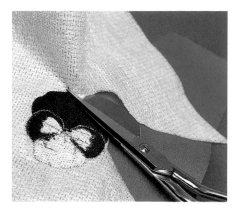

A cut-away stabilizer is perfect to use with embroidery and is easily removed with a pair of scissors.

Cut-Away Plus stabilizer is the perfect weight for making individual appliqués. You can tack these decorations onto clothing to create a three-dimensional effect, and they can be easily switched from one outfit to another (great for fast-growing kids).

I like to embroider a design on a shirt and then top it with the same design done in three dimensions, attaching the appliqué just at the center of the design. To do this, either place one layer of stabilizer in the hoop and embroider directly on it, or place a fabric on top for color. When the design is finished, simply cut out close to the embroidery.

Cut-Away Soft 'n Sheer can also be used to create three-dimensional effects. Simply place one layer of Soft 'n Sheer in a hoop and embroider directly on it. Since the stabilizer is made of very sheer nylon, you can use a wood-burning or stencil-cutting tool to burn it out, leaving no hard edges and no tiny thread ends around the appliqué embroidery.

Stabilizers allow you to machine-embroider on delicate silks and sheers.

Wash-Away Stabilizer

Lyla Messinger

W ater-soluble stabilizers are used to stabilize fabrics in seconds without time-consuming pinning. Like other stabilizers, wash-aways eliminate the annoying shifting, sliding, and puckering of fabric. The excess then tears away easily, and any remaining stabilizer can be dissolved later in water. My favorite brand is Design Plus, a paper product that is transparent enough to allow you to easily trace pattern pieces, gridlines, and designs.

Wash-away stabilizers work well for appliqués, paper-pieced quilt templates, machine embroidery, design transfers, heirloom sewing techniques, and the mesh-fabric technique used in the latticework vest project on the facing page.

USING A WASH-AWAY STABILIZER

It is important to use a stabilizer that is firm and won't shift as you work. It must be stable enough to maintain the pattern of your sewing project and also strong enough to withstand the handling necessary to work at your machine.

When you have completed the sewing for your project, simply tear away as much of the stabilizer as possible and rinse the fabric in water. The remaining paper dissolves in approximately 30 seconds, leaving no residue or stiffness. However, be sure to test a sample piece of fabric before using this stabilizer, to ensure that the fabric is washable. If it can't be moistened to remove the excess stabilizer, then choose a different material for your project.

LATTICEWORK VEST PROJECT

This latticework vest features what I call a mesh effect, constructed from bias-cut fabric tubes woven into a loose open grid. I use a pattern specifically designed for bound edges, which requires no adjustments for the mesh-fabric construction. Since the edges of the mesh fabric need to be bound with bias binding to finish, it is necessary to remove the seam allowance from the edges if you choose a pattern not designed to be bound. However, you should have a seam allowance anywhere the mesh-fabric pattern piece needs to be joined to another pattern piece.

Materials

> Water-soluble stabilizer
> Fabric for the vest
> Vest pattern
> Binding attachment for your sewing machine
> Bias tape maker (optional)
> Tube turner (optional)

1 To prepare the stabilizer, use a pencil to trace each vest pattern piece onto the stabilizer. Cut out the pieces, leaving at least a 1-in. border beyond the pattern's cutting lines.

2 Draw your desired gridlines on one vest side. The vest shown on p. 80 uses a 1½-in. grid pattern.

3 To keep the lattice symmetrical from vest side to vest side, lay the unmarked vest side on top of the marked vest side, and trace the gridlines to the second side. Once you have made these markings (which will be on the wrong side of the paper), you may wish to transfer the markings to the front side of the paper for better visibility.

4 To cut the fabric for the bias tubes, use a rotary cutter and a ruler. Cut strips diagonally across the entire width of the fabric. Since all the strips you need will be fairly short, you shouldn't have to make continuous bias. Different strip widths will create different meshes. For the ¼-in. tube used in this vest, cut generous 1-in. strips.

5 To make the bias strips, use a bias tape maker or the Bias Buddy, a tool which allows you to press the strips, fold them in half lengthwise to form a tube, and stitch at your machine. Using a tube turner, such as the Fasturn, is another quick and easy way to create tubes. Simply sew bias strips of fabric right sides together and turn them right side out with the correct size turner.

My favorite method is to use a binding attachment or foot that will take a flat strip of bias, double-fold the strips, and stitch it together, all in one step. (Be sure to check the binder-foot instructions. Some binder feet will fold the fabric twice for you; others require you to use prefolded bias strips.)

6 Begin by laying two strips on the marked piece of stabilizer, one cross-wise and one lengthwise. Do the longest gridlines first to ensure that you have enough long strips for the areas where you need them. It is difficult to center the strips over the marked gridlines, so align the strips by laying their edges along the marked lines. To keep mirror-image pairs (such as the fronts of a vest) symmetrical, place strips to the left of the gridline on one side and to the right on the other.

7 After the bias tubes have been placed on the stabilizer, join the finished tubes at the cross point. To do this, you can use straight or decorative machine stitches or motifs, or you can hand-stitch if you want the joins to be invisible. Choose the stitch according to your equipment. An electronic machine with an auto-stop control makes it simple to do one decorative stitch and stop; if your machine doesn't have that feature, choose a straight stitch sewn at an angle across the join. Practice your stitch choice on a sample before you start working on the real thing.

STITCHING THE VEST STRIPS

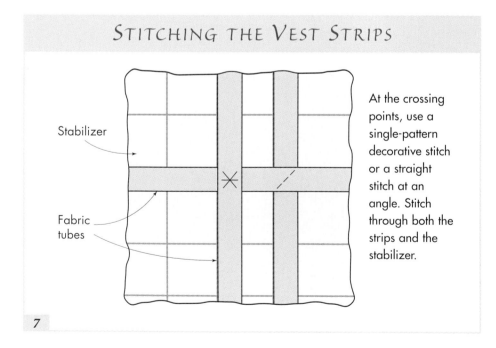

Stabilizer

Fabric tubes

At the crossing points, use a single-pattern decorative stitch or a straight stitch at an angle. Stitch through both the strips and the stabilizer.

7

8 Add the next strip in either direction, making sure that you alternate weaving the crosswise and lengthwise strips over and under each other. Each time the strips cross one another, stitch them down. Continue adding strips, and cut off the excess. Place the leftover strips in a second pile, to be used later on the short gridlines. Continue in this fashion until your mesh is complete.

9 Add a decorative strip to the top of the fabric, if desired. Lay a completed strip on the mesh, and edgestitch it in place. This stitching will attach it to the mesh fabric underneath where it crosses the strips.

10 To finish the fabric, straight-stitch just inside the pattern's cutting line to hold the bias tubes in place along the edge. Then cut away the 1-in. border.

11 When the mesh fabric is complete, sew the garment following the usual order of construction, sandwiching the mesh between a lining or facing and the fashion fabric on all pattern pieces that join the mesh. This would mean the shoulder and side seams for the vest shown.

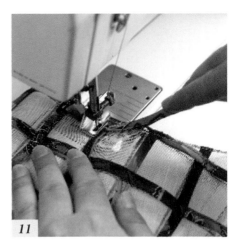

11

Any mesh edges that won't be sewn to another pattern piece need to be bound with bias binding, which can be continued to bind the nonmesh edges as well. The binding will need to be edgestitched for the mesh fabric, rather than stitched in the ditch. A binding attachment will work just as well.

To apply binding to the edges of the mesh fabric using the binding attachment, simply insert the edge of your mesh fabric into the opening between the two layers of the bias strip as you sew.

12 When the sewing is complete, tear away as much of the water-soluble paper as possible.

13 Place the mesh fabric in a sink full of water to remove any remaining paper. Both cool and warm water work well, but warm water works faster. If necessary, gently agitate the mesh to remove the paper. The fabric may also be placed in a lingerie bag and washed in a washing machine on the gentle cycle.

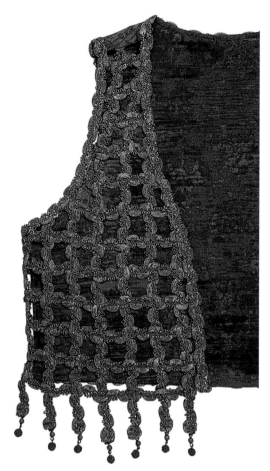

This vest was made using the same technique as the latticework vest but with a decorative green trim in place of bias fabric tubes.

In addition to vest fronts, mesh works equally well for inserts, overlays, or even an entire fabric piece. To fold out some slightly shaped areas of your pattern, simply fold the stabilizer paper in a dart fashion. The mesh drapes softly due to the bias cut of the tubes and will mold over the body.

A faster way to construct a unique variation of the open-weave mesh is to use trim in place of the bias tubes. Preshrink the trim as you will treat the finished garment, and then trim away about ¼ in. outside of the pattern line marked by the straight-stitching along the edge.

Instead of binding, try sewing the wrong side of the trim to the wrong side of the finished mesh fabric along the edges. Turn the trim toward the right side of the garment, and edgestitch the loose edge in place. Then add some beads to the bottom of the strips to create the crowning touch.

USING TRIM AS BINDING

Wrong side

First row of stitching

Right side

Trim folded to outside of vest.

Second row of stitching, close to edge

Trim, right side up

Pattern cutting line (stitched)

Horsehair Braid

Susan Khalje

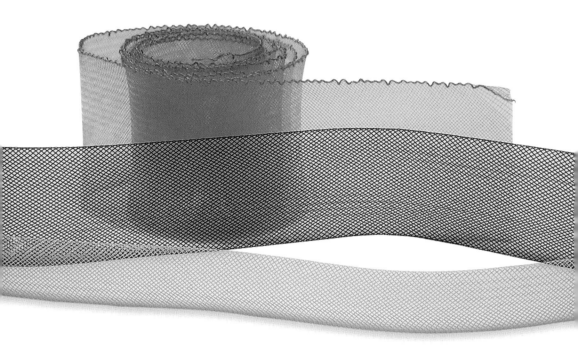

orsehair braid is an under-used yet versatile ally that provides strength behind the scenes. Often referred to as braided horsehair or, simply, horsehair, it adds form, structure, flair, shape, and beautifully uncrushable curves to a garment. In addition, horsehair braid can be compressed without adding thickness; the plastic strands simply squeeze closer as the horsehair narrows.

Although once woven from actual horsehair, today's version of horsehair braid is woven from nylon. It comes in an assortment of colors and weights, in widths of ¼ in. to 8 in. Sometimes a decorative metallic thread is woven in, and the wider forms often have a gathering thread along one edge. A narrow, lightweight version of horsehair is also available, but its effectiveness is limited to hems.

Pleated horsehair doesn't have any specific technical uses but is spectacular for decorative purposes.

USING HORSEHAIR BRAID

Although horsehair can be used decoratively—as surface adornment, as a semitransparent band joining two pieces of fabric, and in millinery—its uses within a garment are even more varied.

Horsehair along hems

Most sewers are familiar with the placement of horsehair along hems, especially in wedding gowns, where it adds definition to the hemline for a dramatic, defined silhouette. Horsehair is often machine-stitched along the hemline of a wedding dress, just

HORSEHAIR ALONG A HEMLINE

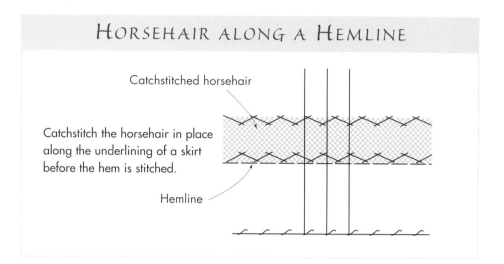

Catchstitched horsehair

Catchstitch the horsehair in place
along the underlining of a skirt
before the hem is stitched.

Hemline

within the hem allowance. The edge is
then folded along the hemline and
pressed, sometimes with the addition
of a narrow strip of fusible tape to
keep it in place against the fashion
fabric.

The nature of horsehair encourages
it to stay as pressed even without the
addition of tape; tacking the horsehair
to the seam allowances is usually
enough to keep it in place. It can be
stabilized further by machine stitching along the hemline, a scant distance from the edge. The stitching is
barely visible, and not only will it
thoroughly anchor the horsehair and
position it as desired, but it also adds
further definition to the hemline.

Horsehair can be placed inside the
hem allowance of a relatively narrow
skirt to help strengthen and define its
lower edge. Since there's no great
weight or strain on the horsehair,
loose basting stitches (applied by
hand) can hold it in place.

Wide horsehair can be used to
exaggerate the flare of a skirt; to

HORSEHAIR WITH A GATHERING THREAD

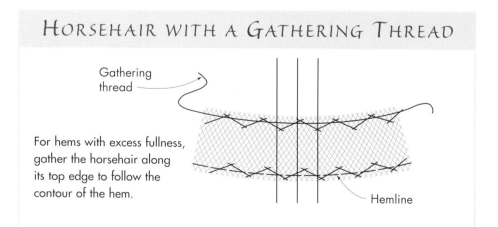

Gathering
thread

For hems with excess fullness,
gather the horsehair along
its top edge to follow the
contour of the hem.

Hemline

Hems can be shaped with horsehair of various widths, from narrow—to lend subtle definition—to wide—to encourage a dramatically shaped hem to stay in place.

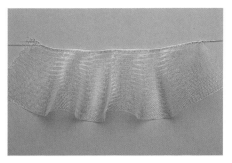

Wide horsehair has a gathering thread along one edge, which can be used to shape the horsehair to match the contour of the hem.

accommodate the flare, pull the gathering thread along its top edge to shape the horsehair. Similarly, horsehair can be used to define and strengthen applied ruffles and flounces. It is also the perfect tool to define a fishtail hem, since the horsehair can be easily shaped to fit the curve of the hemline.

In these cases, applying the horsehair by hand will give you the most control over its shaping and placement. And even if it doesn't have a gathering thread to help you shape it, you can easily apply one by hand or machine; this thread will work as well as one that's been added by the manufacturer.

Other ways to use horsehair

Aside from using it on hems, horsehair has many uses in other supporting roles:

- Horsehair can be stitched, usually by machine and often in multiple rows, onto an underskirt, lending support to a

skirt from beneath. The horsehair supports the garment without altering the movement of the fashion fabric.

- Horsehair has often been used in couture clothing inside horizontal pleats. A lightweight fabric, cut on the bias and formed into pleats, gains form and flare from the horsehair resting within the folds of the pleats.

- Nothing supports a bow like horsehair. When forming a bow from a flattened tube of fabric, insert horsehair of a compatible width inside the tube. The horsehair flares to shape the outer curve of the bow, yet compresses flat in the center where the fabric gathers or folds.

Horsehair used inside a bow both strengthens it and provides added fullness.

HORSEHAIR INSIDE A COLLAR

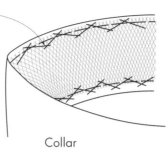

Loose catchstitch

Wide horsehair supports the curve inside a collar or inside an off-the-shoulder sleeve.

Collar

- Horsehair can be used as a gentle form of boning. Two narrow strips of horsehair machine-stitched together in a zigzag pattern are much firmer than a single layer and can help shape stand-up collars.

- Design details that stand away from the body—off-the-shoulder sleeves and portrait collars, for example—are helped enormously by the presence of horsehair. Catchstitch the horsehair in place to an inner layer. (In the case of off-the-shoulder sleeves, be sure the ends of the horsehair are incorporated into the stitching line that joins the sleeve to the armscye; otherwise, the horsehair will help shape the sleeve but won't be able to hold it firmly out from the bodice.) After stitching the horsehair into the seamline, trim it and bind the seam allowance; this keeps the sharp plastic ends of the horsehair from working through the fabric and disturbing the wearer.

- Horsehair can also be used to make sleeve heads. For particularly heavy sleeves that can't be supported by anything else, several layers of strong horsehair, stitched together and folded into pleats, can be manipulated into strong, unbendable sleeve heads.

Tip

If horsehair has been used along a hemline and is exposed, its cut ends will have to be covered. You may be able to tuck the ends into the garment's seam allowances, but it's best to overlap the ends, covering the join with a fabric patch or a piece of ribbon. Be sure the patch is strong enough to keep the raw edges from working through, since they can be very uncomfortable against the skin.

Horsehair is catchstitched in place behind the lace for a sleeve that stands away from the body.

Boning

Susan Khalje

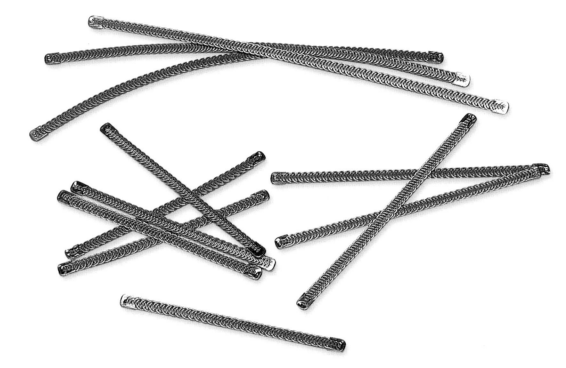

Boning is an essential element for garments that are off-the-shoulder, strapless, or built up at the waist. Without it, these types of garments don't have the necessary body support to counteract the natural tendencies of gravity and the strain of movement. Well-placed and carefully applied, boning can make the difference between a garment of uncertain engineering and one that is comfortable to wear, is soundly constructed, and stays in place.

There are three types of boning from which to choose:

- **Plastic boning,** available in all fabric shops, is the easiest to find. It's sold along with a fabric casing, which is sewn into the garment. One advantage of plastic boning is that it can be cut to any size, but I find that, apart from small applications, it lacks a good deal of strength.

- **Rigilene** is another type of boning that's relatively easy to find and can also be cut to size. It doesn't need a separate casing; it's made from a series of tiny little plastic strips, which can be stitched through. The disadvantage is that once the boning is applied, the garment becomes cumbersome to work with.

- **Spiral-steel boning,** my favorite type, is strong yet lightweight and flexible. It is ¼ in. wide and is available in ½-in. increments, from 2 in. to 17 in. long. It's also available by the pound, but I find it difficult to cut and even harder to tip (round off the ends). I prefer to stock a range of sizes or order what I need.

USING SPIRAL-STEEL BONING

When you think of boning in a garment, what usually comes to mind is a strapless gown or bustier. These garments, more than almost any other, need the extra support provided by boning. When positioned properly, boning is invisible and absolutely comfortable, so use it freely for added structure.

Boning in strapless bodices and off-the-shoulder dresses

Boning is essential on strapless bodices. Place it in the bust area, either along the princess seams or from the top of the princess seam straight down, somewhat to the side of the bust. Running boning directly over the bust is tempting but can cause unnatural stiffness; however, this technique is sometimes successful when the garment is well fitted in the bust area. You can also place boning along the side seams to straighten out the seams, thus eliminating puckering and elongating the silhouette. The same is true of boning used along the back of a garment; place a piece of boning every few inches, from the top edge to the bottom edge.

On a laced-up bodice, tension can cause horizontal pull lines. To prevent the sagging that spoils the decorative effect of the lacing, use a piece of boning on either side of the opening. This will eliminate the pulling and keep the bodice fully stretched vertically.

Highlighting the presence of boning on the outside of a bodice is an attractive look. Sometimes the topstitching on the fashion fabric is all we see; other times a separate fabric tube is sewn to the surface of the garment. Either way, it's critical to experiment to get the correct width for the boning channels; it's also important that the ridges from the spiral-steel boning aren't visible.

BONING PLACEMENT IN A STRAPLESS BODICE

This strapless bodice uses 11 bones, placed strategically along the center front, under the bust, alongside the bust, at the side seams, and along the back for support.

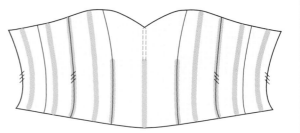

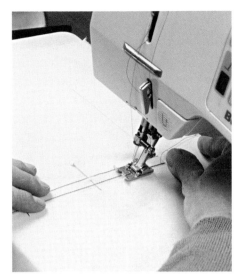

Boning channels are easily made from silk organza. A ¼-in. bone requires a ⅜-in. channel, which is then stitched to the underlining or over a seam allowance along the same stitching lines as the channel. The boning is inserted after the construction of the garment.

Boning channels can be purchased, but it's quick and easy to make your own. For a ¼-in. bone, sew a ⅜-in. channel from silk organza. Ribbon can also be used, but one of the challenges of working with boning is to conceal its presence; sewing a strip of ribbon onto the underlining doesn't add a layer of camouflage the way a fabric tube does.

If you're simply topstitching on the surface of the garment, be sure that your stitching experiments mimic exactly the layering of the bodice. Boned bodices are usually made from several layers of fabric, which may prevent adding layers of underlining; the fabric in the seam allowance will usually provide all the padding you need. It's best to stitch on these channels by hand, as you'll have more control than if you sew them on by machine.

On an off-the-shoulder dress, boning is placed much the same as on a bodice. Its most critical position on the dress is from the high points of the bodice (usually where the bodice's uppermost points join the armscye at the front and back) all the way down to its base.

Other uses for boning

Boning also has a range of unorthodox uses, thanks to its unyielding nature, which can be an enormous asset "behind the scenes." Other garment areas that benefit from boning include:

- **The horizontal edge of a square neckline.** It's easy to hide a piece of boning in the seam allowance,

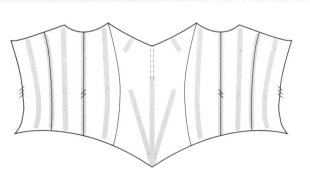

BONING PLACEMENT IN AN OFF-THE-SHOULDER BODICE

Here, 15 bones are used. Notice that none of the bones is used directly over the bust, which can cause unnatural stiffness.

Boning for basque waists varies, depending on the shape and depth of the V. Strengthen and hold down the point of a basque waist (A) with three bones; a dropped waist (B) should be stabilized with boning used all the way to the base of the bodice.

A

B

between the fashion fabric and the facing.

- **High waistbands.** Without some sort of internal support, a high waistband can sag. To prevent this, place a few pieces of boning inside, perpendicular to the waistline.

- **Pants with a "Hollywood" (or built-up) waist.** An extended waistline is beautiful but requires a separate waistband. Boning can be applied to darts and seam allowances; the garment will stay in place with a waist stay to link the boning.

Tip

When pressing boned garments, be careful not to ruin your careful work of application and camouflage. Using a pressing cloth is not good enough. A better solution is to press the boned area face down into a terry towel.

- **A V waist.** Boning is essential to keep a V waist in place. Three pieces of boning, running down into the base of the V and fanning out up into the torso (stopping short of the swell of the bust) will keep the V from distorting.

- **Turned-back cuffs.** Wide, turned-back cuffs will be encouraged to keep their shape if the cuff area is supported with a little boning. Position it perpendicular to the bottom edge of the cuff.

- **Shoulder straps.** Sometimes the weight of a garment will pull side shoulder straps out of shape. Small pieces of boning, placed horizontally, will spread out the fabric and eliminate vertical pull lines.

- **Stand-up collar.** Short pieces of boning, arranged vertically, will keep a stand-up collar in place.

Fusible Stay Tape

Lyla Messinger

Fusible stay tapes are a "must have" sewing notion. They not only simplify your sewing but also fine-tune the finished look of a garment. The more you use fusible stay tapes, the more uses you'll find for them!

There are two types of stay tape: fusible bias stay tape and fusible straight stay tape.

Fusible bias stay tape, which is cut on the half bias, provides a controlled amount of stretch that is useful for curved edges and easing. It is perfect for quick curved necklines and hem edges, armscye control, knit shoulder stays, fabric fray, and stretch control. Fusible straight stay tape is commonly used for jacket roll lines and shoulder stays, and for stabilizing edges like the tops of pockets, long edges, and more. Both types of tape are lightweight, ⅜ in. wide, and available in either white or black.

Fusible straight stay tape is used in the roll line of this jacket to define and stabilize where the collar turns back.

USING FUSIBLE STAY TAPE

Before using fusible tapes on your garment, always test-fuse a fabric sample first. Fusing time will vary depending on the type and thickness of the fabric, as well as the iron's temperature (use a setting appropriate for the fabric being used). Remember to protect the fabric with a press cloth, then wash it in cool water or have it dry-cleaned.

Fusing is a simple process:

1 Press the fusible tape to the wrong side of the fabric, with the fusible side down.

2 Obtain a permanent bond by applying steam, heat, and pressure with an iron. You can use a steam iron, or you can lay a damp press cloth over the tape and apply heat and pressure with a dry iron.

3 Fuse for approximately 10 seconds to 15 seconds.

Curved necklines without facings

One of my favorite techniques for using bias stay tape is creating curved necklines without facings. Before I started using fusible stay tape, making a curved neckline without facing often resulted in a stretched, twisted edge. Try the following procedure to create a controlled neckline that is fused in place before stitching, to prevent shifting and twisting. Using this technique, the neckline will remain stabilized for the life of the garment because the tape stays in place permanently.

1 Serge the tape to the neckline, fusible side up, on the wrong side of the garment. If you have a ⅝-in. seam allowance, cut off ¼ in. of the neckline fabric as you serge. Use a narrow serger stitch with a little-longer-than-normal stitch length. This will ease the fusing, by allowing as much as

An asymmetrical neck edge keeps its shape, even without a facing, when you stabilize it with fusible bias stay tape.

possible of the tape's fusible adhesive to be exposed.

If a serger is not available, trim ¼ in. off the neck edge before applying the tape. Overcast or zigzag the tape to the garment neck edge, as described above. Try not to stretch the tape as you stitch it to the neck; you will need the give in the bias cut of the tape when you press.

2 Lay the garment wrong side up on the ironing board. Using only the tip of the iron, press the taped neck edge to the wrong side of the garment in an up-and-down pressing motion. Work a small section at a time. Ease the curve into shape with your fingers as you work. You can use pins to hold the eased fabric in place, but don't press on them because they may leave a mark on your garment. Instead, try placing the point of the pin into the serged edge, through the garment, and into your ironing-board cover.

Tip

To make straight necklines without facings, use the technique described in the instructions for making curved necklines without facings. Apply straight stay tape in place of the bias; all other steps remain the same.

3 Stitch the neckline in place permanently from the right side of the garment. Use a longer-than-normal stitch length and a single or double needle.

Armscye control

A common complaint about vests and sleeveless garments is gapping in the armscye over the bust. Gapping can be caused by the shape of the bustline and distortion due to fabric stretching. This curve can be eased by using fusible bias stay tape.

1 Mark your pattern piece above and below the bustline at the armscye. Transfer the markings to your fabric.

2 Place the garment right side down on the ironing board. Fuse the bias tape ½ in. from the edge, fusible side down, stretching it slightly in the bust areas between markings as you fuse.

3 Stitch ⅛ in. into the tape as you attach the facing or lining. The majority of the tape will be in the body of the garment and will stabilize the curve for the life of the garment.

To prevent distortion due to fabric stretching, trace your pattern piece onto pattern tracing paper. Lay your new pattern piece on the ironing board. Immediately after cutting your fabric pattern piece, lay it on top of the paper pattern piece, right side down, before you fuse the stay tape in place. You can now be sure that you have the correct shape and size for the piece.

V-neckline control

A creative way to use fusible straight stay tape is on a V-neckline. This tape has a slight amount of give that allows you to stretch it as you fuse, easing in the neckline to hug the body.

1 Working at the ironing board with the fabric wrong side up, fuse the tape ½ in. from the neck edge.

2 Use a pattern piece traced on pattern paper, as described above, to ensure the correct shape and size through the neck area.

3 Working several inches at a time, lightly pull on the tape, pressing it onto the fabric surface, and fuse in place. This will ease the fabric, and the finished result will be a neck edge that hugs the body instead of gapping out.

4 Stitch through ⅛ in. of the tape as you apply the facing or lining. This leaves the majority of the tape in the body of the garment, where it remains for the life of the garment.

Grosgrain Ribbon

Susan Khalje

As simple and unassuming as grosgrain ribbon may appear, its presence is often essential to the inner workings of a garment. Grosgrain has a variety of decorative as well as structural uses. Usually woven in a combination of rayon and cotton, grosgrain is a firm, sturdy, ribbed strip of fabric. Real grosgrain ribbon is identified by tiny scallops along both edges and is difficult to find. But it's worth searching out; it has qualities that are lacking in other grosgrains (those with woven ridges, not scallops, along their edges).

Although available in a number of widths, 1-in.-wide grosgrain is the most versatile. It's wide enough to be strong but not so wide that it becomes bulky. A good source will have grosgrain in a range of colors.

USING GROSGRAIN RIBBON

Beyond its decorative uses, grosgrain is most essential as an internal tool. I use it mainly in traditional waist-bands, as a shallow waist facing, and as a waist stay, among other things.

Traditional waistband

Grosgrain can be used during the early fitting stages to help determine the exact location and circumference of the waistline. The same piece of grosgrain can later be positioned in the garment. Measuring and placing it carefully early on will allow you to use it accurately later.

To use grosgrain in a traditional waistband on a skirt or a pair of trousers, follow the steps on the facing page.

1 Place a row of staystitching along the garment's waistline, easing the fabric a little if extra fullness needs to be drawn in.

2 Hand- or machine-baste the lower edge of grosgrain to the seam allowance, along the staystitching line.

3 Stitch the fashion-fabric waistband to the garment along the waistline, enclosing the grosgrain inside. The garment now hangs from the grosgrain, which functions as a waist stay, and the fashion-fabric waistband is set so that it will not become distorted. You can also extend the grosgrain ribbon into the waistband's underlap, strengthening that as well.

Shallow waist facing

Grosgrain also makes a beautiful shallow waist facing. It's a lightweight treatment that's quick and easy to apply—perfect for a simple skirt that rests at the waistline. One of the essential qualities of grosgrain ribbon is its ability to be shaped by steam, in this case, to conform to the contours of the garment's waistline. In fact, you'll be amazed at how easily it can be manipulated. Follow these instructions to create a waistband facing:

1

1 Superimpose the grosgrain over the pattern tissue (or the top edge of the garment), and shape it with the steam and heat of your iron.

2 Prepare the garment by staystitching the waistline and treating the raw edge of the seam allowance.

3 Place the edge of the grosgrain on top of the seam allowance, along the staystitched waistline, and stitch close to its edge.

4 Clip the seam allowance generously, and fold the grosgrain into place. Press it, and tack it at darts and seam allowances.

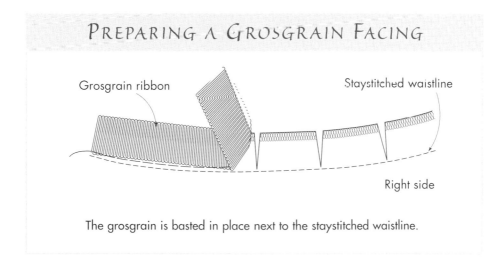

PREPARING A GROSGRAIN FACING

Grosgrain ribbon

Staystitched waistline

Right side

The grosgrain is basted in place next to the staystitched waistline.

5 Turn both edges in at the opening, or extend the grosgrain on one side to form an underlap. Use a snap to hold the underlap in place.

Grosgrain as a waist stay

Grosgrain is also a wonderful waist stay. A "stay" is a piece of fabric—often narrow—that acts as a stabilizer. A bias-cut neck edge can be "stayed," for example, with a narrow ribbon, to keep it from stretching; an inner stay placed at the waistline of a garment can act as an unseen support.

In the case of high-waisted pants without a separate fashion-fabric waistband on the outside (but with

Grosgrain is used as a stay inside a contoured waistband to help keep it from stretching.

inner boning to support and strengthen the built-up waist), a grosgrain waist stay adds essential inner structure. Supporting the garment from within, it attaches to the seam allowances and the boning channels along the waistline, and fastens separately from the garment.

A grosgrain waist stay is also an essential component of a boned bodice. While the boning holds the

> **Tip**
>
> Buttonholes in the lining, reinforced with small squares of silk organza, make good openings for a grosgrain waist stay.

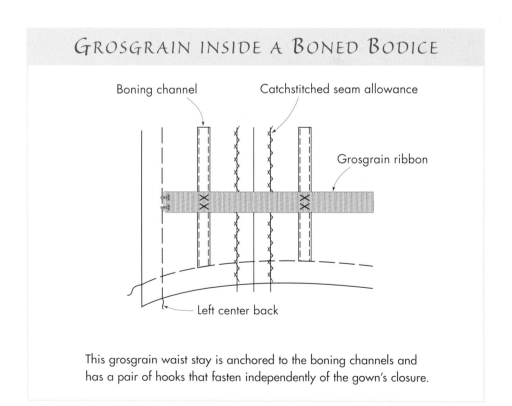

GROSGRAIN INSIDE A BONED BODICE

Boning channel

Catchstitched seam allowance

Grosgrain ribbon

Left center back

This grosgrain waist stay is anchored to the boning channels and has a pair of hooks that fasten independently of the gown's closure.

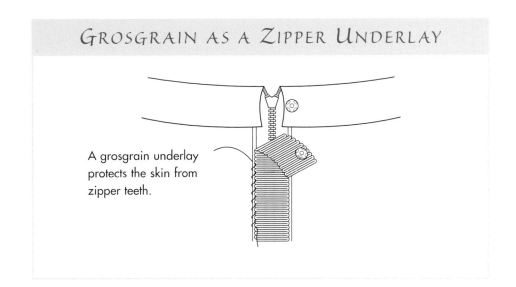

A grosgrain underlay protects the skin from zipper teeth.

fabric taut, it's the grosgrain stay that anchors the boning and forms the baseline from which the boning rises.

The grosgrain waist stay is tacked to each boning channel and closes separately from the garment. Its presence is often camouflaged by the garment's lining, so in order to fasten, small openings must be made in the lining for its ends to emerge. In addition to providing support for the bodice, a grosgrain waist stay, when used in conjunction with a heavy skirt, provides the anchor from which the skirt hangs, sparing the bodice and the shoulders the full weight of the garment.

Other uses for grosgrain

• Sometimes, strapless or off-the-shoulder garments are fashioned with a sewn-in foundation—a boned inner corselette—which shares only a common upper edge with the garment. It stops at the waist, closing separately from the garment, while its bottom edge is anchored with a grosgrain waist stay.

• Grosgrain ribbon can also be used cosmetically as a zipper underlay. It serves as a buffer between the zipper teeth and the wearer. Simply hand-stitch the grosgrain in place along one side of the opening and along the base of the zipper, to the seam allowance. Keep the remaining edge of the grosgrain in place with a small snap at the top of the zipper placket.

Temporary Spray Adhesive

Pat Welch

T emporary spray adhesives are a good alternative to pins. Spray adhesive holds two pieces of fabric tightly together so that stitching can occur without the movement of either fabric. It was originally developed for appliquéing, with excellent results; when the temporary adhesive disappeared, a soft appliqué was left, instead of the hard, stiff appliqué so often seen with bondables.

Not all spray adhesives are created equal. My favorite, KK 2000, is formulated with highly concentrated material and a heavier-than-air propellant. You can reposition the fabric for about three hours after it is applied, and the adhesive disappears completely in three to five days. KK 2000 does not gum up the needle, as some other spray adhesives do, and it requires only one short spray, going directly where it's aimed. Compared to the flammable butane-propelled adhesives, which need two or more cloud-producing sprays, KK 2000 is the only safe, nontoxic, nonflammable, ozone-friendly spray on the market.

USING A TEMPORARY SPRAY ADHESIVE

Thanks to creative experimentation by sewers, I've found that there are many fantastic uses for the spray. Anywhere you would normally use pins, consider using a temporary spray adhesive instead. Here are some instances when I use spray adhesive:

A temporary spray adhesive holds this narrow piece of trim firmly to the fabric without pins, so there is no movement as you sew.

- Holding stabilizers in place for tight-as-a-drum hooping.

- Holding "unhoopables," such as collars, cuffs, and pockets, in place on the stabilizer.

- Sewing trims, lace, or any second layer.

- Hemming. Spray the hem of slacks, skirts, and jackets and fold up. Check the length, and hand-hem, blindstitch on the machine, topstitch, or double-needle topstitch. You will have perfect hems every time since there is no movement between the layers as you sew, which can occur with pins.

- Holding a pattern on the fabric when cutting it out.

- Applying zippers with no stretching.

- Quilting. For pinless, puckerless machine quilting, simply spray the backing and place the batting on; then spray the batting and place the top on, and sew. No more safety pins every 6 in.

- Holding patches in place while stitching.

- Stenciling.

- Holding shoulder pads in place.

Clear Elastic

Sue Hausmann

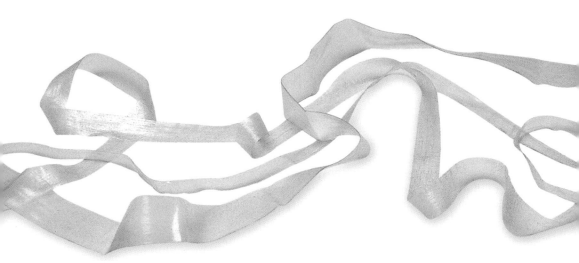

1 'm always amazed by how many people have never heard of one of my favorite notions, clear elastic. Clear elastic is a great notion for quick finishing and quick fixes, because it encourages garments to retain their original shape with soft flexibility. I prefer it to using regular elastic because clear elastic is very soft and supple and does not add bulk or thickness to the garment. I have enough bulk already!

> **Tip**
>
> A word of caution: Do not buy more clear elastic than you can use in a year, because all elastics weaken with age.

Clear elastic is stretchy, lightweight, and made of polyurethane, and can be purchased in a package or by the yard in widths of ¼ in., ⅜ in., and ½ in. I purchase all my elastics in quantities of 15 yd. to 25 yd.

USING CLEAR ELASTIC

When stitching through elastic on your sewing machine or serger, always increase the stitch length. Too short a stitch will sew the stretch out of the elastic and defeat the purpose of sewing it in. It's also good to stretch the clear elastic once before using it, to remove any excess stretch.

Applications
for clear elastic

Some of my favorite applications of clear elastic include using it on shoulder seams, armholes, necklines, sleeve hems, and neck ribbings, as well as for easing heavy fabric without adding bulk. For all these techniques, I use ⅜-in. elastic.

- Stitch clear elastic along the edge of any neckline, sleeve hem, or other garment edge that tends to stretch out or gap. On some garments, I actually eliminate the neck and armhole facings, set my Huskylock serger for standard 3-thread sewing, stitch length 3 to 4, and serge clear elastic to the wrong side of the neck edge.

  If the neck needs to be "controlled," stretch the elastic ever so slightly as you serge. Once the elastic is in place, fold the elastic to the wrong side and topstitch the edge with a twin needle on your sewing machine or a serger cover stitch.

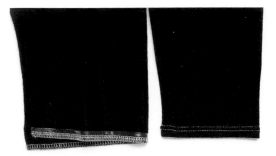

With elastic serged to the wrong side of the hem and then topstitched, these sleeves won't loose their shape when they're pushed up.

I especially like this technique for hems in long sleeves that will be pushed up. Often the sleeves slip down, and the edge becomes stretched out. Follow the steps above to serge clear elastic to the wrong side, then fold the hem to the wrong side and topstitch with a twin needle or a serger cover stitch. The elastic holds the sleeve in place when it's pushed up, and also remembers the original size and shape of the sleeve edge.

- Stitch over clear elastic when sewing the shoulder seam, especially on knit garments. This will tape the shoulder to keep it from stretching out but will retain the soft flexibility of the fabric.

Clear elastic can be placed on the wrong side of neck and armhole edges to prevent stretching and gapping.

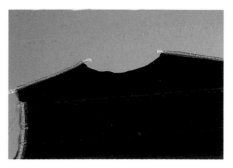

Clear elastic in the shoulder seams of knit garments strengthens without adding stiffness.

- I love using clear elastic to ease heavy fabric without adding bulk. Sometimes two rows of long stitching do not work well for gathering or easing, as with a heavy coat fabric or a raw-silk sleeve cap.

  In this case, measure a length of clear elastic on the bodice pattern, front and back, marking the shoulder and other markings. Place elastic on the sleeve cap, match the markings, and set your sewing machine for a straight stitch at a 4-stitch length (6 stitches per inch [spi]). Stitch the elastic to the sleeve cap, stretching it so the markings match. The sleeve cap is now eased to the perfect size to sew into the garment.

To keep necklines and wrists from stretching out, use clear elastic along the ribbing foldline.

Even hard-to-ease fabrics can be eased to the perfect size with clear elastic.

- Clear elastic is a perfect way to keep neck ribbings from stretching out as a result of wear and washing. This is especially important when using self-ribbing (ribbing cut on the crossgrain or bias of a stretch fabric); since the fabric is not as elastic as actual ribbing, the strip usually must be longer.

  After cutting the ribbing strip for the neckline and wrists, cut a piece of clear elastic the same length. On the wrong side of the ribbing strip, place the clear elastic lengthwise along the center. When sewing the ribbing into a circle, catch the ends of the elastic in the seam to anchor them. Sew the ribbing to the neckline and wrists. The clear elastic will stay right at the fold of the ribbing to keep it from stretching out.

- When armholes or necklines have stretched out from wear, stabilize and reshape them with clear elastic. Get between the facing or lining and the outside of the garment to the seam allowance of the stretched-out area. Lay clear elastic on the seam allowance and stretch the elastic as you sew, using a zigzag stitch set at a long stitch length (4mm/6 spi) and narrow width (2–3). The more the garment gaps, the more you stretch. This has saved many an outfit for me.

MOCK TURTLENECK

I love the look of a turtleneck, mock turtleneck, or ribbed neckline under a blouse or sweater but find that it is often too warm to wear. This "mock turtleneck" has no sleeves and so adds designer detail without the warmth. It also eliminates the waistline bulk because it does not go all the way to the waist. You've seen them in designer catalogs; now you can make them quickly and easily.

Materials

Your favorite T-shirt pattern
½ yd. of knit fabric
Ribbing (or extra knit fabric for self-ribbing)—3 in. for a crew-neck, 5 in. for a mock turtleneck, 10 in. for a turtleneck
⅜-in. clear elastic, 2 yd. to 3 yd.

1 Measure the length from the shoulder to just under the bust and add ½ in. Cut the front and back pieces of your T-shirt to this length. (Note: For a fuller bust, cut the front ¾ in. to 1 in. longer than the back and ease the extra length into the side seam.)

2 Sew the shoulder seams using a seam/overcast stitch for knits on your sewing machine or a 3- or 4-thread serger stitch. To tape the seam, stitch clear elastic on the wrong side along the edge of the armholes.

3 Sew the side seams. Stitch elastic to the bottom edge as you did with the armholes. You can leave the serger finish because the elastic is soft against the skin, or you can turn the elastic to the wrong side and topstitch.

4 Try pulling the neckline over your head. Cut it larger, as needed, so it pulls easily over your head. Cut the ribbing using a rotary cutter, a ruler, and a rotary cutting board. Here are some guidelines for cutting the ribbing (these will vary depending on the amount of stretch in the ribbing and on your personal preference):

For width, cut the ribbing strip 2½ in. to 3 in. wide for a crew neck, 4½ in. to 5 in. wide for a mock turtleneck, or 9 in. to 10 in. wide for a turtleneck. Experiment with different widths or measure a favorite shirt.

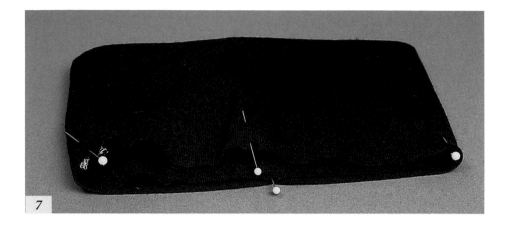

For length, measure the neckline. Cut ribbing two-thirds the length of the neckline measurement or, for self-ribbing, three-quarters the length. Pull the strip of ribbing around your head for a final fitting and trim off the excess.

5 Cut a piece of clear elastic the same length as the ribbing strip.

Tip

If your sewing machine or serger balks at stitching the elastic to the fabric, start sewing on the elastic only, then raise the presser foot and place the fabric under the elastic. Lower the presser foot and sew.

6 Stitch the ribbing into a circle with a ¼-in. seam allowance, and add the elastic to stabilize, as in step 2.

7 Mark the neckline and ribbing into quarter markings, as shown. Pin the ribbing to the neckline, matching the markings.

8 Stitch the ribbing to the neckline, using a seam/overcast stitch on the sewing machine, or a 3- or 4-thread serger stitch. (I find ¼-in. seam allowances the easiest to work with.) Sew with the ribbing on the top, stretching it as you sew to match the neckline. When sewing the ribbing with a serger, set the differential feed between 1 and 2 to ease the neckline onto the ribbing.

Double-Sided Fusible Tape

Lyla Messinger

U ltra-soft Double-sided Fusible tape (UsDsF) is another "must have" sewing notion in my studio. This paper-backed web is nearly impossible to detect after fusing in place, and it doesn't gum up the needle when sewn through. It is best used as a fabric stabilizer or whenever two pieces of fabric need to be permanently attached to one another.

USING DOUBLE-SIDED FUSIBLE TAPE

Before using double-sided fusible tapes on your garment, always test-fuse a fabric sample first. Fusing time will vary depending on the type and thickness of the fabric, as well as the iron's temperature (use a setting appropriate for the fabric being used).

Remember to protect the fabric with a press cloth, then wash it in cool water or have it dry-cleaned.

As with fusible stay tape, it's important to test-fuse fabrics before using them on your garments. Fusing time will vary according to fabric type, thickness, and iron temperature, which you should set according to the fabric you're using. Remember to use a press cloth to protect the fabric, which should then be washed on cool settings or dry-cleaned.

You'll obtain the best results if you fuse as follows:

1 Press the paper-backed adhesive to the wrong side of the fabric with a dry iron, just long enough for the adhesive to attach to the fabric.

2 Peel the paper away from the adhesive. The adhesive layer should remain on the fabric.

3 Obtain a permanent bond by applying steam, heat, and pressure with the iron. Fuse for 6 seconds to 10 seconds.

With your iron, you can use this fusible to:

- hem fine fabrics
- control knit hems
- create fusible trim and bias tubes
- position zippers
- match plaids and stripes
- tack facings
- stabilize buttonholes

Invisible hems

Using UsDsF, it's possible to hem silks and other fine fabrics without sewing them. It stays soft, and it does not change the feel or drape of your fabric.

1 Serge or clean-finish the hem edge.

2 Press UsDsF in place ¼ in. from the hem edge on the wrong side of the fabric. Use the edge of the serger stitching or the clean-finish as a guide.

3 Pin the hem in place. Remove the paper.

4 Remove the pins, then press the hem ¼ in. from the edge. Do not apply pressure to the serged or finished hem edge at any time, leaving your hem completely invisible and without unsightly ridges.

Double-needle knit hem

Commonly seen in ready-to-wear, this hem finish for knit fabrics has always been one of my favorites. Because the double-needle stitch forms a zigzag

pattern on the wrong side, it has built-in give, which works beautifully with a knit. UsDsF acts as a stabilizer when making this hem finish. In the past, the hem finish was hard to do because the hem had a tendency to stretch out of shape with the double-needle stitching. By fusing first, the hem will not stretch when stitched.

The technique is very easy; as an added bonus, the adhesive in the finished garment stretches with the fabric, as if the tape weren't there at all. Stretchy knits are best stitched, however, rather than simply fused. UsDsF prevents stretching and shifting as well as loose stitches when hemming knits. The fusible moves with the fabric as it is worn, while the stitches secure the hem.

To use the tape for hemming a knit with a double needle:

1 Fuse the hem as described in the instructions for the invisible hem.

2 Using a long stitch length (3½ to 4), stitch the hem from the right side with a 2.5/75 or 4.0/75 stretch double needle. Stitch through the UsDsF to keep the fabric layers from shifting, as well as to prevent stretching and loose stitches. You may also use a serger

2

cover stitch instead of the double needle on the sewing machine, if it is available on your overlock machine.

Fusible trims

For any nonraveling fabric like knits, Ultrasuede, or Facile, UsDsF makes a quick and easy fold-over trim.

1 Fuse UsDsF in place on both sides of the inside of the fold-over trim. An easy way to mark the placement of the edge of the trim is to stitch a line on the garment with water-soluble thread. Placing the trim along this line of stitching on the inside and outside of the garment ensures an even trim on both sides of the garment.

2 Remove paper from one side of the trim. Fuse the first side of the trim in place on the garment edge. Avoid pressing the second side.

3 Remove the paper from the second side of the trim. Fold the trim over the edge of the garment, and fuse in place.

4 Spray water on any visible water-soluble thread marking to remove after the binding is complete.

5 Straight-stitch along the edge, or get creative and use a decorative stitch along the edge.

Fusible bias tape or tubes

Decorative uses for fusible trim are endless. Apply UsDsF to the wrong side of trims, remove the paper, and the trims will curve and bend to any shape you like. You'll have a much larger selection of fabrics from which to choose than those available in manufactured trims.

Fusible bias tape is simple to make.

1 Press single-folded bias strips using a bias tape maker.

2 Fuse UsDsF to the wrong side of the strips, being careful to cover both raw edges where they meet in back. Fuse carefully to avoid stretching the bias as you apply the fusible.

3 Remove the paper backing, and apply bias strips to the fabric. The paper will not bend in a curved shape, but the fusible web will.

This fringed, self-fabric trim was attached with double-sided fusible tape, which is soft enough to let the fabric form decorative curves.

Fusible bias tubes are created in a similar manner. After making the tubes, fuse UsDsF to the wrong side of the tube when it is straight, being careful not to stretch it. If UsDsF is too wide, simply trim it with a rotary cutter or scissors to the desired width before fusing.

Tip

Keep in mind that if the fabric stretches farther than the adhesive, it may pull loose where there is stress in a garment. These areas should be avoided or stitched through.

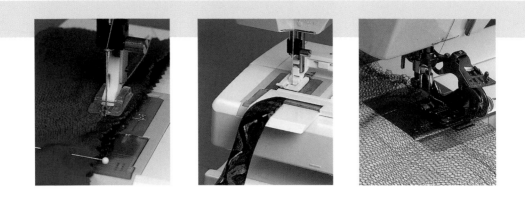

part FIVE

f you've ever been frustrated by having the thread snap while trying to gather a ruffle or by burning your fingers while folding and pressing bias tape, the notions in this chapter can help. The machine accessories discussed here are specialized notions that allow even the most basic sewing machine to accomplish complicated techniques. You'll be amazed at what you can do with these additions to your sewing bag of tricks.

From the basic bias tape maker, which helps to produce prefolded bias seam binding in a fabric of your choice, to the Fastube Foot, which lets you evenly and effortlessly sew bias tubes of any width, these notions are great time-savers that free you for more creative endeavors.

ine Accessories

Elastic Wizard

Gayle Starbuck and Jan Grigsby

T he Bonfit No Hands! Elastic Wizard takes all the stress out of applying elastic. This valuable tool stretches the elastic and reliably gives even, consistent gathers. It may be used for any task that requires applying elastic directly onto a project, as well as for some applications that use a casing. Most types of elastic work well; however, knit elastic is the easiest to use because of its stretch. It also has holes for the needle to stitch into, which avoids breaking the rubber threads.

USING THE ELASTIC WIZARD

To apply the elastic directly onto a project, simply snap the Wizard foot onto your sewing machine, and choose the correct guide for the size of elastic being used. There are six guides (⅛ in., ¼ in., ⅜ in., ½ in., ¾ in., and 1 in.), which reflect the size of the elastic you're planning to use, and a tension screw on each guide. Set the tension screw on the elastic guide for the amount of gathering desired, and then sew on a scrap of the project fabric, using a multistep zigzag, regular zigzag, or straight stitch.

Applying elastic to a cut-on waist-band is just as simple. Clean finish the edge of the garment and apply elastic on the wrong side, ¼ in. down from the finished edge. To complete the casing, fold it over and stitch with a zipper foot along the edge of the elastic.

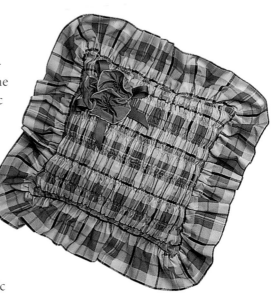

RUFFLED, SMOCKED PILLOW

This simple project uses a plaid fabric and is a good way to get the feel of using the Elastic Wizard. Use ½-in. seams throughout.

Materials

1 yd. of cotton plaid
Matching thread
12-in. by 12-in. pillow form
3 yd. of ⅛-in. knit elastic
¾ yd. of 1½-in. wired ombre ribbon
½ yd. of ⅝-in. moss green satin ribbon
Bonfit No Hands! Elastic Wizard

1 Cut the fabric according to these specifications:

- pillow front: 1 rectangle, 13 in. by 24 in.
- pillow backs: 2 rectangles, 11 in. by 12 in.
- ruffle: 2 strips, 7 in. by 44 in.

2 Using the marking tool of your choice, mark smocking lines on the wrong side of the pillow front. The lines should be 1½ in. apart, except for the top and bottom lines, which should be 1¼ in. from the top and bottom.

MARKING SMOCKING LINES

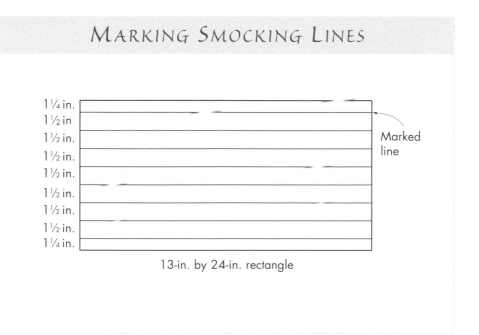

1¼ in.
1½ in
1½ in.
1½ in.
1½ in.
1½ in.
1½ in.
1½ in.
1¼ in.

Marked line

13-in. by 24-in. rectangle

3

3 Apply the elastic using tight tension on the elastic guide, following the marked lines. Stretch each previous line to keep the gathers consistent.

4 Press on the right side. Trim the pillow front to a 13-in. by 13-in. square, and staystitch ½ in. from all raw edges. Trim all threads and elastic ends as necessary.

5 Sew the ruffle-strip ends, right sides together, to form a circle. Fold in half lengthwise, wrong sides together, and press. Gather, using your favorite method.

6 Divide into quarters, and pin in place.

7 Baste and then stitch, carefully allowing plenty of fullness at the corners.

8 With one of the 11-in. by 12-in. rectangles, turn under ½ in. on one 12-in. edge. Turn under another 3 in. and press. Hem.

9 With the right sides together, place the pillow back on top of the pillow front, overlapping the pillow backs and sandwiching the ruffle in the center. Pin at the corners and every few inches, keeping the edges aligned. Baste, catching the ruffle evenly.

10 Sew together, using a ½-in. seam allowance.

11 Clip the corners and trim the seam as necessary, then turn and press. Remove all basting stitches that show, and insert the pillow form.

12 To make ribbon rosettes, cut the wired ombre ribbon into three 4-in. lengths. Remove the wire from one edge of each length and hand-gather. Pull the gathers into a circle and overlap the ends. Hide the raw edges and secure them with hand stitches.

12

13 Cut the satin ribbon into five 4-in. lengths. Make three loops, basting the ends together. Place the rosettes onto the pillow as desired, and stitch them in place.

14 Tuck the loops under the rosettes, and stitch in place. Stitch the remaining ribbons under the rosettes for the stems, and stitch in place. Trim the stem ends at the angle desired.

Ruffler

Mary Morris

A t first sight, a ruffler attachment for your sewing machine can be more than a little off-putting Resembling a small metallic insect, the attachment ranges in price from around $20 to nearly $70, depending on the brand of your machine. Don't be deterred! If you have a home-decorating, costume, or dress-making project requiring ruffles, the ruffler attachment will very quickly prove to be worth its weight in gold.

Specific manufacturers vary the design, but all rufflers operate in essentially the same way. Rufflers are actually tiny pleaters. Unlike gathers, the pleats cannot be adjusted once they have been sewn, so this attachment is not suitable for such tasks as gathering sleeves or a full skirt to fit a bodice.

USING THE RUFFLER

The stitch selector, usually on the top of the attachment toward the front, can be set to make a tiny pleat on every stitch, every sixth stitch, or every twelfth stitch. It also can be set to bypass the pleating altogether. The depth of the pleats can be adjusted with a small circular dial below the stitch selector. Tiny, finger-like pieces of metal make the pleats by gently shoving them into place under the needle on the designated stitches.

Rufflers are designed so that the fabric to which the ruffle will be attached can be placed under the entire attachment, which allows you to both ruffle and assemble in one operation. I do not recommend this, however, when working with net (as in the petticoat project included here), but it's great for making a bed ruffle or attaching a single decorative ruffle to the bottom of a full skirt.

Before beginning any ruffling project, cut a sample piece of the fabric you'll be using and test it at various pleat settings. For the petticoat project, I set my pleater to pleat on every stitch at the maximum depth—2½ in. of fabric pleated down to roughly 1 in. This setting will vary from one project to another depending on the desired amount of fullness. On slightly heavier fabrics—such as cotton for a dust ruffle on a bed, or satin to adorn a dress—the pleats need not be as deep to produce the same effect as that on a lighter fabric.

PETTICOAT PROJECT

This petticoat is a prototype of one that I designed and mass-produced (17 of them!) in two days. It features interior ruffles to provide the added fullness often required by square-dancing, ballroom-dancing, and period-ballet designs. The tiers ensure that the fullness is added below the high hip and at the hemline, where it is most needed, and not around the waist, where it can be most unflattering.

Additional fullness at the hem can be created by adding fishing line inside the ribbon trim along the edge of each bottom ruffle and/or horsehair braid along the inside of the inner ruffle. The ribbon trim is to prevent the raw edge of the net from catching the dancer's stockings or tights (the net is too stiff to take a good rolled edge on a serger).

The following petticoat will have a finished length of approximately 22 in. To make a longer petticoat, a fourth ruffle can be added, which would require a longer innermost ruffle and an additional short ruffle inside of it. The length of each tier can be adjusted to achieve fullness closer to the waist, if desired. Fabric allotments would then need to be recalculated, based on the fact that each tier will be approximately 2½ times greater in circumference than the one above it.

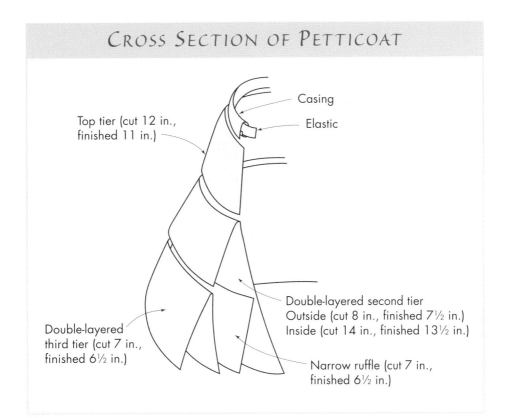

CROSS SECTION OF PETTICOAT

Top tier (cut 12 in., finished 11 in.)

Casing

Elastic

Double-layered second tier
Outside (cut 8 in., finished 7½ in.)
Inside (cut 14 in., finished 13½ in.)

Double-layered
third tier (cut 7 in.,
finished 6½ in.)

Narrow ruffle (cut 7 in.,
finished 6½ in.)

Materials

- 4¾ yd. of 55-in.-wide cancan nylon net (without the interior ruffles, 3 yd. is sufficient)
- 27½ yd. of 1-in. (or wider) satin ribbon (craft ribbon is not appropriate), or 7 packages of double-fold bias tape in a matching or contrasting color (without the interior ruffles: 8 yd. of ribbon or 2 packages of double-fold bias tape)
- Waistband elastic three-quarters the circumference of the wearer's waist
- Optional: 27½ yd. of fishing line or fine wire to be inserted into the ribbon trim for extra stiffness and/or 3¼ yd. of horsehair braid to be sewn along the hem of the innermost ruffle

1 Begin by folding the net in half lengthwise, lining the selvages up with the long side of the table. (Cutting on a table with straight edges helps you cut each ruffle evenly.) Place a piece of transparent tape at the desired point (see measurements in step 2) on a flexible transparent ruler, a wooden ruler, or a yardstick.

2 Keeping the edges of the net parallel with the side of the table, place the end of your ruler along the perpendicular edge of the table and pull the net along until the cut edge meets the tape. Cut through both layers along the end of the table according to the guidelines on p. 114:

- Top tier: one piece, 12 in. deep by 45 in. wide (10 in. less than the fabric width)

- Second tier (outside): two pieces, each 8 in. deep, the entire width of the fabric

- Second tier (inside): two pieces, 14 in. deep, the entire width of the fabric

- Small ruffles along the bottom edge: 16 widths of the fabric, each 7 in. deep

3 Using a narrow zigzag stitch (approximately 1½mm wide and 1mm long) and a narrow seam of ¼ in., attach all the sections of each width into one long piece. On the narrowest ruffle, be sure all seam allowances are in the same direction.

4 Attach the ruffler to your machine, following the manufacturer's directions.

5 Insert one edge of each ruffle between the two darker layers of metal. In order not to become entangled in the small, fingerlike "pushers," bring your fabric from the front to the back. You may not be able to begin at the very edge of the fabric.

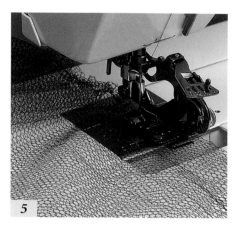

5

6 If possible, set your machine to sew at a slow speed. Make sure the bobbin is full, and then begin ruffling the narrowest ruffle.

7 Match up the top edges of the two layers in the second tier (the outside one being 8 in. deep and the inside one being 14 in. deep), seam allowances to the inside. Ruffle these two layers together. (Note: When stitching the tiers together, begin and end ½ in. from the cut edges.)

8 Fold the narrowest ruffle in half between the eighth and ninth sections, seam allowances to the inside.

9 Beginning at the end of the folded ruffle where you'll find the two cut edges, seam two layers of the narrow ruffle to the bottom edge of the shorter of the two layers of the second tier. Use the same narrow zigzag stitch you used to seam the ruffles. Cut off the excess.

Tip

Even at its deepest setting, the ruffler may not pleat a single layer of net as tightly as two layers. With 2½ times more fabric than your finished length, the leftovers are great for a headdress or neckline accent.

10 Match the unruffled edge of the remaining short ruffle to the side of the longer layer of the second tier, which faces the shorter layer. Top-stitch in place.

11 With the right sides together, stitch the ruffled edge of the two-layered second tier to the bottom of the final tier.

12 Turn a ½-in. hem in to the wrong side along the top of the uppermost layer and stitch. Fold a 1-in. casing to the inside and stitch in place.

13 Insert the elastic through the casing, and staystitch the ends of the elastic inside the casing at either end.

14 Turn the petticoat inside out. For the final assembly, stitch together the raw edges of each layer (turning back the inner seams as needed) in this order:

- all the way down to the outermost layer, from the casing, through the top and second tiers to the bottom ruffle
- the inside short ruffle attached to the shorter layer of the second tier
- the short ruffle attached to the longer layer of the second tier
- the longer layer of the second tier

15 Turn the petticoat right side out.

16 To add the ribbon trim, first iron it in half lengthwise. Inserting the fishing line as you go, place the trim around the edge of each bottom ruffle, and stitch it in place. If you wish to add the horsehair, insert it inside the ribbon trim on the innermost layer as you sew it in place.

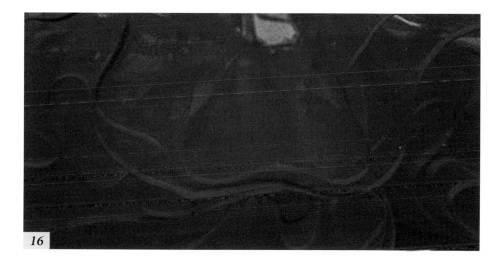

16

Edgestitch Foot

Barbara Deckert

T o avoid my usual wobbly topstitching and edgestitching, my Bernina #10 edgestitch foot allows me to accurately stitch on my commercial machine without my work getting away from me. These feet are available to fit all machine brands, but your machine must have an adjustable needle position, with a minimum of L-C-R positions. The Bernina foot features a flexible metal tongue suspended between the toes of the foot, which is attached at the shank.

USING AN EDGESTITCH FOOT

The edgestitch foot is great not only for edgestitching but also topstitching and for sewing on patch pockets. If your material is bulky, it may not feed easily, but in general the edgestitch foot will work for most applications.

- For edgestitching, simply butt your work up against the left side of the tongue and allow it to guide the fabric under the needle. To change the distance of the stitching from the edge, vary the needle position to the left. Always test a scrap of material to determine the best distance.

- To topstitch, use the tongue like a seam guide. Run the tongue over a previous row of stitching, and adjust the needle position as desired.

- To sew on patch pockets, guide the tongue along the pocket edge and stitch, adjusting the needle position as desired.

Tip

By adjusting the needle position, you can also sew multiple rows of precisely spaced topstitching, which you can use to accent belts, flaps, or collars.

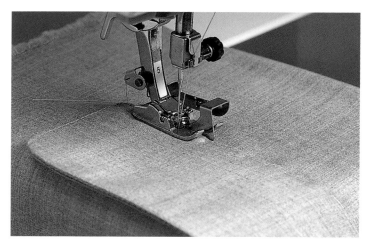

The top of this pocket feeds next to the edgestitch foot to create a straight row of stitching.

Binding Attachment

Connie Long

The binding attachment is a practical and efficient tool that makes it easy to finish edges creatively. Colorful bindings are easily made from strips of lightweight fabric, which are used to enclose the raw fabric edges on garments and home-decorating projects.

Narrow bindings are a wonderful way to create lively seams and edges simply by using a contrasting color or a complementary fabric, but patterned wovens or knits are more fun to experiment with. Look for printed wovens, patterned knits, or jacquard patterns or stripes that, when folded, will create interesting bindings that add color or movement to the edge of the garment. Very often a patterned fabric will have several different repeat designs that can be used to create a number of attractive edges.

USING A BINDING ATTACHMENT

Although the typical binding attachment can be used when binding knits, it is meant to be used with a woven binding fabric cut on the bias. This kind of fabric must be cut on the bias so that the binding can conform to curved edges.

If you are binding straight edges, cut the binding following the crossgrain. Bindings cut on the crossgrain have more flexibility than those cut on the lengthwise grain, but not as much flexibility to follow curved edges as bias-cut bindings.

Knitted binding fabric can be crosswise grain because knits have crosswise stretch and conform to curves as well or better than bias-cut woven binding. The amount of stretch depends on the knitted fabric you are using. If your knitted fabric is very stable, it is best to cut the binding on the bias just like woven binding. You may also find that you like the printed or knitted pattern better that way.

Binding can be used as a functional and decorative way to make reversible garments. Simply sew the garment with a standard seam and then trim and bind the seam allowance with a colorful binding. As a result, one side of the garment will have plain seams, and the other side will have raised bound seams. Finish the outer edges with binding as well, using the same fabric as the plain side of the garment or the decorative binding fabric.

Binding can also be strictly decorative, such as when you create bound tucks in the fabric. To use the binding to create ridges of color, simply fold the fabric where you want to apply the binding to the folded edge. In this case, it is easiest to create the bound tucks before cutting out the garment, because folding and binding the fabric reduces its size. Otherwise, you must allow extra width or length depending on the direction and position of the tucks.

To create binding for a garment:

1 Cut your binding fabric to a width that is compatible with the binding attachment you are using. My binder uses 1⅛-in.-wide fabric strips and creates a binding about ⅜ in. wide.

2 To facilitate feeding it through the binder, cut the binding fabric to form a point at the center. Slide the pointed end of the fabric through the binder using a long pin or an awl. Feed the binding so the wrong side of the fabric is facing you.

2

3 Slide the binding fabric back and forth through the binder to align it, making sure that the folds are even on both sides.

4 Before inserting the garment, begin sewing the binding together for a few inches. This allows you to have more control and also helps the binding feed back at the beginning of the application. The binder folds the

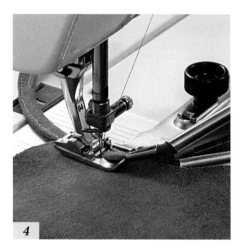

binding fabric into position just before the fabric feeds under the sewing-machine presser foot, so that the folded edges can be stitched in place.

5 If you are binding a neckline, leave one shoulder seam unstitched so that you can apply the binding end-to-end. (You cannot bind a continuous edge or a circle with the attachment.) Close the shoulder seam after applying the binding.

6 Bind the sleeve hems before closing the sleeve, and bind sleeveless garments before closing the side seams.

7 To bind the continuous edge around a cardigan, leave a few inches open near the hem at one of the side seams to start and end the binding at an inconspicuous place.

Bias Tape Maker

Syl Pearson

T he bias tape maker is a simple tool that folds fabric into exact halves for perfect bias. Bias is normally used for the bindings of neck openings, armholes, hems, and blankets. It may also be used for garment embellishments, stained-glass quilting, place mats, and even wall hangings. Bias tape also works for weaving or lattice projects and for finishing needlework and craft projects.

There are a variety of tape makers available to create tape sizes of ¼ in., ½ in., ¾ in., 1 in., and 2 in. Each tape maker is color-coded on the top and back (the grooved area), and the size is written on the front of the tape maker. The resulting tape comes out of the flat section and is always accurate in size and never varies in width.

On each package, there are two fabric measurements given for tape-strip sizes: one for medium-weight fabrics and the other for thin, lightweight fabrics. For variety in your bias bindings, try using lamé, tissue lamé, eyelet, decorator fabrics, satins, brocades, and, of course, calicos of all colors and prints.

USING A BIAS TAPE MAKER

A bias tape maker is very easy to use.

1 To create the strips or bias tape, cut the fabric either vertically or horizontally, depending on the end use. If the strips are to be used in a project that requires no curving, they may be cut vertically; if they will be used in a project that requires curves, cut the fabric diagonally (45 degrees).

> **Tip**
>
> To do the actual cutting, use a rotary cutter, a mat, and a straightedge guide or ruler. These tools make the cutting much faster and more accurate.

2 Guide the fabric strip into the tape maker. You may need to cut the fabric into a point and force it through the tape maker using an awl in the center groove.

3 Put the tape maker on an ironing board with the shiny surface down and the handle and the grooved side facing up. Place a pin on the end of the folded fabric to secure it to your ironing board.

4 Pull the tape maker by the handle while ironing the folded tape as it exits the flat end.

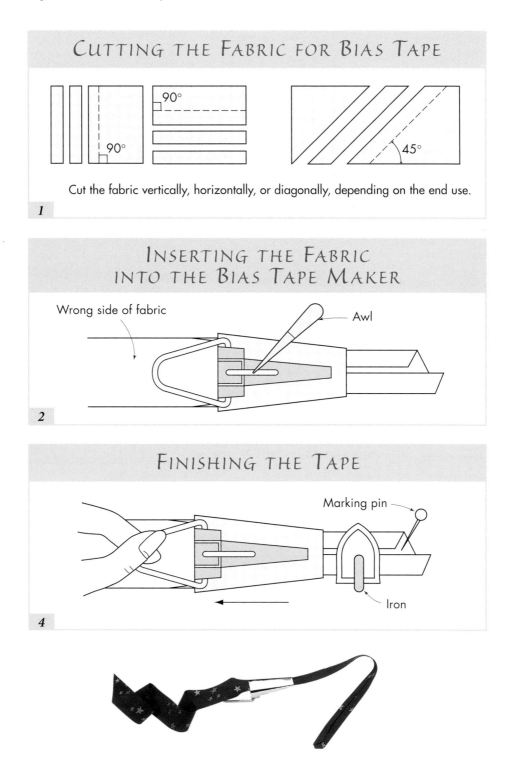

CUTTING THE FABRIC FOR BIAS TAPE

90°

90°

45°

Cut the fabric vertically, horizontally, or diagonally, depending on the end use.

1

INSERTING THE FABRIC INTO THE BIAS TAPE MAKER

Wrong side of fabric

Awl

2

FINISHING THE TAPE

Marking pin

Iron

4

Fasturn

Emma Graham

The Fasturn makes turning fabric tubes fun and easy. It is a hollow brass cylinder with a specially designed wire hook that allows you to fill fabric tubes with cord, batting, or wire at the same time they are turned. Fabric tubes are then easily sewn into quilts, vests, dolls, accessories, crafts, embellishments, and fabric weaving.

The Fasturn set includes six cylinders ranging in size from ⅛ in. dia. to ¾ in. dia., with three different-size wire hooks. A smaller version of the Fasturn, the Miniturn, contains three tubes of small diameters—⅛ in., 3⁄16 in., and ¼ in.—that are each 6 in. long. The Miniturn is designed for miniature projects, such as button loops and jewelry embellishments, where only small amounts of fabric are needed.

For turning fabric tubes that are large, long, and bulky, the Blue Tubes are ideal. The diameters of these tubes are 1 in., 1¼ in., and 1½ in., and they come in two lengths—12 in. and 18 in. The Blue Tubes make easy work out of creating tube quilts, dolls, place mats, vests, and home-decorating projects.

USING THE FASTURN

The amount of fabric that will fit on a cylinder varies depending on the type of fabric, the size of the fabric tube, and how tightly the fabric fits on the cylinder. Most cylinder sizes will take between 2 yd. and 3 yd. of bias-cut fabric and about 1 yd. of straight- or crossgrain-cut fabric.

1 Cut a fabric strip, either on the bias or straight of grain. The Fabric Cutting Reference table, shown here, is calculated for cutting bias strips only.

Fabric Cutting Reference–Bias Strips			
Cylinder	Diameter	Fabric Cutting Width	Finished Tube Width
1	⅛ in.	1 in.	³⁄₁₆ in.
2	³⁄₁₆ in.	1¼ in.	⁵⁄₁₆ in.
3	¼ in.	1½ in.	⅜ in.
4	⅜ in.	1¾ in.	½ in.
5	½ in.	2¼ in.	¹³⁄₁₆ in.
6	¾ in.	3 in.	1⅛ in.

For straight-of-grain strips, add ⅛ in. to ¼ in. extra to the cutting width. I recommend using bias-cut strips on the #1 and #2 cylinders and trimming the seam to ⅛ in. before turning the #1 tubes.

2 Fold the fabric strip in half lengthwise, right sides together, and stitch with a ¼-in. seam. You have now created a fabric tube.

3 Insert the Fasturn cylinder (of the appropriate size) into the fabric tube, pushing the entire fabric tube onto the cylinder. You can bunch up the fabric tightly to fit.

4 Fold the end of the fabric tube over the cylinder opening about ½ in., and hold it in place. More than ½ in. may cause too much bunching inside the cylinder as it is pulled. Less may result in the wire hook tearing out of the fabric.

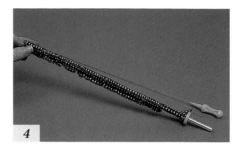

4

5 With your other hand, insert the wire hook into the cylinder opening and pierce the fabric. Hook through the entire thickness of fabric in the center to keep the wire from ripping out of the fabric. If the hook point penetrates the fabric close to the edge, the threads may be pulled apart, releasing the hook.

6 Twist the wire handle to the right until the wire-hook pigtail is completely through the folded-over fabric.

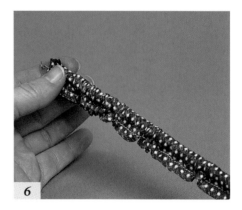

6

7 Hold on to the wire handle and, without twisting, pull the handle and the wire straight back to draw the fabric into the cylinder about 1 in. Do not twist it; twisting to the left releases the wire hook from the fabric. If the hook comes out, try rehooking it by twisting the handle to the right.

8 With your fingers, press the seam open a couple of inches. The seam will stay open if the fabric is not pushed too fast, and will be easier to press flat later.

9 With your other hand, ease the fabric tube down the cylinder while pulling back on the wire handle. Push and pull at the same rate. Once the fabric tube comes out of the cylinder's handle end, release the wire hook by twisting to the left.

10 Continue to ease the fabric as the other hand pulls the end of the fabric tube completely through the cylinder. Your fabric tube is now turned.

10

🅣🅘🅟 To turn a longer fabric tube, leave an opening in the center side seam, and stitch the ends of the tube closed. Insert the Fasturn cylinder through the opening and reach up to turn one end at a time, pulling back through the opening.

How to turn and fill a fabric tube

The Fasturn also allows you to fill a fabric tube at the same time it is being turned. There are many kinds of filler for tubes: cording, yarn, cable cord, paper craft cord, strips of polyester or cotton batting, chenille wire, stiff belt backing, and mop strands. All of these will work, but do not try to pull something through the cylinder that is larger than the opening, unless it is soft and compressible. Experiment first with small pieces to get the size you need.

Turning and filling at the same time is an easy operation.

1 Begin by setting up your fabric as in the previous instructions, until the end is tucked into the cylinder about 1 in. (step 7).

2 Open the seam and, with your fingers, press it open for a couple of inches. This will allow the seam to fold smoothly around the fill.

3 Lay your fill on a smooth table or flat surface. Touch the end of the cylinder (with the tucked-in ends) to the end of your fill, and continue turning the tube.

4 As you pull back on the wire handle, the fabric at the bottom end of the cylinder will grab onto the fill and pull it inside as the tube is being turned.

If your filler piece is too short for the tube, simply pull the filler all the way into the fabric tube, stopping when it is just inside the end of the cylinder. Add a dab of tacky glue to the end of the filler and add another piece of filler to the glued end. Then continue turning and filling.

CHRISTMAS ANGEL ORNAMENT

Materials

6-in. by 45-in. white/gold fabric
1½ yd. trim
4-in. gold picot trim (for halo)
1 yd. of ¼-in. ribbon
Pins
Glue
Pin board or ironing board
Fasturn set, or #4 Fasturn
Optional: Fastube Foot

1 Cut or tear three fabric strips, 2 in. wide by 45 in. long, on the straight of grain. Cut ribbon into 6½-in. lengths.

2 Fold all 2-in.-wide fabric strips in half lengthwise, right sides to right sides. Sew a ¼-in. seam on the long side to create a tube. (For quick, easy, and accurate tubes, use the Fastube Foot on your sewing machine.)

3 Turn tubes with the #4 Fasturn, and open the seam as you start turning. This will make it easier to press the seam flat.

4 Press the tubes flat, with the seam centered on an outside edge.

5 Cut the tubes into 6½-in. lengths.

6 On a flat surface, such as a pin board or large ironing board, lay 9 or 10 tubes horizontally and close together, to create about a 6½-in. square. Pin the ends in place.

7 Flip every other tube back to approximately the center of your square. Use your pins to hold them in place temporarily.

8 On each tube remaining flat, place a dot of glue along the center-line. Using another 6½-in. tube, lay it vertically across the top of the glue-dotted tubes, centering it in your square. Make sure this tube is pulled taut.

9 Place a dot of glue on top of the new vertical tube, in the area where the other tubes are flipped back.

10 Fold down the flipped-back tubes over the new vertical tube and glue dots. To adhere, press the tubes down with the palm of your hand.

11 Flip back the alternate tubes to the edge of the previously placed vertical tube. Lay a 6½-in. piece of ribbon

> *Tip*
>
> You can make your tubes using two different fabric strips. Adjust the cutting width to allow for a ¼-in. seam on each side, and be sure to stitch in the same direction.

vertically, snug against this fold-back line. Fold down the flipped-back tubes over the ribbon, adhering with glue as before.

12 Continue this flip-and-glue technique, alternating tubes and ribbons, until the full 6½-in. square is woven. Let it dry for 15 minutes.

13 Pin the angel pattern to the top of the woven square. Carefully carry the woven section to your sewing machine. Using a regular straight stitch, sew a line around the angel pattern, close to the outside edges.

14 Remove the pattern piece. Cut the outside edges close to the stitching.

15 Glue the decorative trim around the edges of your angel to hide the raw edges of the tubes and the ribbon. Pin it in place until the glue dries.

16 After one side is dry, flip the angel over and glue the decorative trim as before. Add a piece of gold picot trim to create a halo before you finish gluing trim on the angel's head. Tuck the halo edges under decorative trim to hide the raw edges.

17 For a hanger, add a short piece of ribbon and tuck the raw ends under the decorative trim of the angel's head. Or, using a needle, run a heavy gold thread through the top of the angel and tie it in a knot.

ANGEL PATTERN

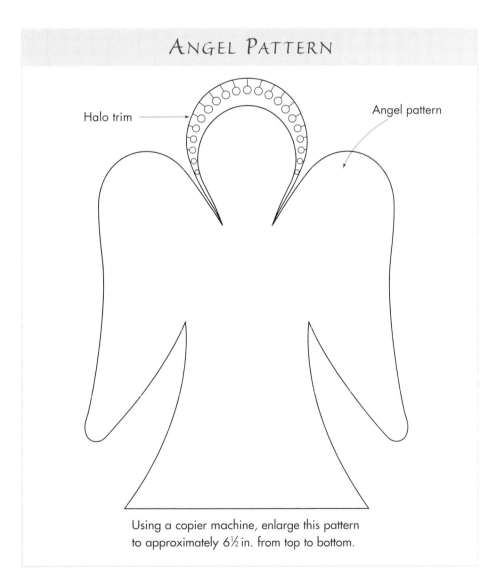

Halo trim

Angel pattern

Using a copier machine, enlarge this pattern to approximately 6½ in. from top to bottom.

Fastube Foot

Emma Graham

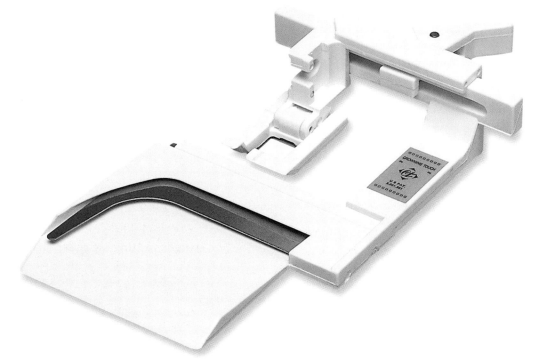

The Fastube Foot is the perfect accessory for sewing fast, easy, and accurate fabric tubes. It folds the fabric strip and sews and measures tubes accurately from the fold of the fabric to the seam. There are five versions of the Fastube Foot, with two adapters available, to fit most sewing machines.

USING THE FASTUBE FOOT

The Fastube Foot is designed to be used with light- to medium-weight fabrics, which move easily through the foot. When you press the seams open on joined bias strips, they slide through the Fastube Foot with little problem.

Heavy fabric seams may need some assistance. If the seam is too thick for the guide, lift the presser foot and gently pull the fabric through; then lower the presser foot and resume sewing. When all the tubes are sewn, remove the Fastube Foot and stitch the seam openings with a regular presser foot.

To slide and adjust the foot for tube size, simply unlock the lever located on the back of the foot and adjust according to the size tube you want to make. After adjusting the foot, lock it into position again. With the Fastube Foot, you can make straight-of-grain or bias tubes anywhere from ⅛ in. to 1½ in. wide. If you're using the foot in conjunction with the Fasturn, consult the "Perfect Tubes Guide" (sold separately) to adjust the stitching position quickly and easily for each size Fasturn cylinder. Now you're ready to sew miles of tubing, all the same width.

1 When stitching bias strips, set your sewing machine for a short stitch and a very slight zigzag (between 0 and 1). This helps prevent thread breakage while turning and gives a bit more flexibility to the tube.

2 Cut the end of each strip at a 45-degree angle, with the point at the right corner. Slide the point underneath the metal flange.

3 Fold the left half of the fabric strip over the top of the metal flange and push under the needle, aligning the side edges of the strip evenly. When set properly, your seams will be approximately ¼ in.

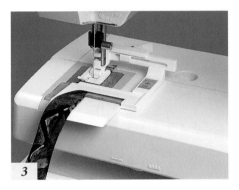

4 If you are using a Fasturn, sew a few inches and then test the fit on the appropriate Fasturn cylinder before finishing your tubes. You may have to readjust the foot slightly, if the fit is too tight or too loose.

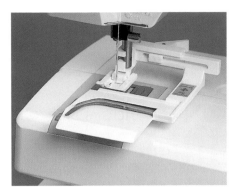

The lever at the back of the foot can be adjusted and locked to make tube sizes from ⅛ in. to 1½ in.

Longer fabric tubes may require fabric lengths to be joined together (see the drawing below). To do this, join the bias strips by cutting the ends of each strip at a 45-degree angle. With the right sides together, stitch ¼-in. seams, then press them open and trim the edges even with the strip.

Tip

Chainstitching saves time when sewing several strips into tubes. Stitch one strip, sew a couple stitches, and start the next strip (without cutting the thread in between), and so on. When you are finished sewing strips, go back and cut the connecting stitches to separate the tubes.

MAKING LONG FABRIC TUBES

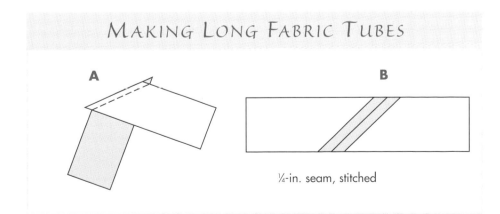

A

B

¼-in. seam, stitched

Universal Presser-Foot Lifter

Emma Graham

T he Universal Presser-Foot Lifter is every sewing artist and quilter's dream. This unique and innovative tool attaches to almost all sewing machines, both new and older models. It lifts the presser foot, freeing your hands to control the fabric for pivoting and adjusting. Also included is a nonslip platform for your sewing machine pedal, which can be positioned right next to the Universal Presser-Foot Lifter pedal. Shifting from one pedal to another is as easy as driving a car, leaving your hands to the more important job of precisely controlling your fabric.

There are four versions of the pedal, to fit most machines, and four different connector clamps that attach to the sewing-machine lifter arm. The cable, equipped with stick-on receivers and cable anchors, is long enough to wrap around the front of the sewing machine and down to the platform. The receivers are designed so that you can remove just the cable anchors and detach the Universal Presser-Foot Lifter for use on another machine. The receivers stay in place, allowing for easy attachment and removal.

Velvet V Foot

Clotilde

S ewing a silk or rayon velvet dress can be a most frustrating experience; you may even determine that you'll never sew that fabric again. The problem is a result of the short, hair-like fibers of the pile fighting each other as the presser foot stitches the seam. The fabric creeps and bunches up, resulting in an ugly, rippling seam. In addition, the pile is flattened by the pressure of the standard foot, which results in an unattractive look.

The solution is the Velvet V Foot, long used in garment factories and now finally available for home sewing machines. The underside of the foot is flat except for a narrow ridge that touches the fabric. The foot itself "floats" on top of the fabric. (This is the same principle used by sailboats that float on the surface of the water with only the keel submerged.) Due to the narrow strip of contact, there is no pressure to push the fibers against each other, thus eliminating "creeping." You can now have a perfectly flat, even seam.

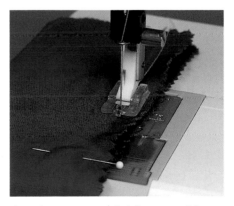

The Velvet V Foot rests lightly on top of the velvet, preventing the nap from being flattened along the seamline.

Tilt'able

Anna Zapp

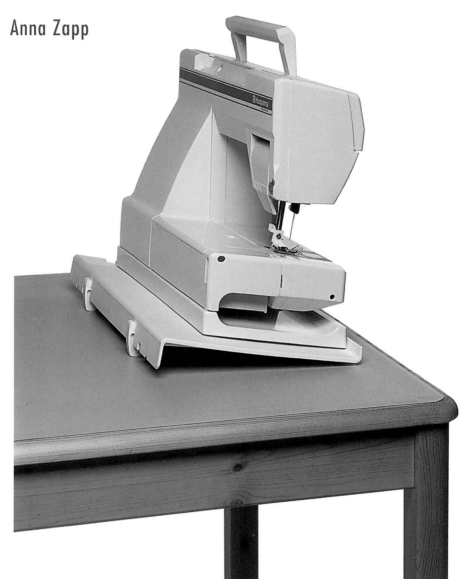

T he Tilt'able is a plastic, angled platform that may look insignificant, but can have a big impact on your sewing enjoyment. Not only did it take a herniated disk in my neck but also the advice of a physical therapist and extensive research and development to create this small table, which has since saved me years of neck, shoulder, and back strain commonly associated with sewing.

At the sewing machine, we traditionally lean over a flat surface to clearly see the needle and what we're sewing. Many sewers become so involved with their projects that they don't move for long periods of time, staying hunched over in an unnatural position. To make matters worse, our movements are repetitive, causing even more strain on the muscles.

The Tilt'able is designed to tilt your sewing machine forward at an angle, allowing you to sit up straight at the machine rather than hunching over it. The tilt also provides a significantly improved view of the needle and sewing tasks. The end result is a more comfortable posture that prevents muscle pain and strain, and lets you do precision sewing, serging, machine quilting, appliqué, and embroidery even more accurately than before.

The SureFoot System is a companion to the Tilt'able. This footrest has a nonskid mat on the bottom, which prevents sliding, and a grooved surface that locks the sewing-machine pedal and footrest into place. The SureFoot System keeps both feet together and level on the floor and balances the hips, ultimately preventing the lower-back pain that many sewers experience.

USING THE TILT'ABLE

The Tilt'able is designed to accommodate all machine brands and adjusts to six different angles. The lowest tilt setting is specifically designed for Bernina sewing machines. All other machines work well on any setting, so choose the one that gives you the best view of the sewing area, taking into consideration factors such as the height of your sewing table and chair. You don't have to worry about your

fabric sliding off the machine because your presser foot will hold it firmly in place.

If your sewing machine is in a cabinet or on an extension table, the Tilt'able can easily adjust to either situation. For cabinets, simply lower the cabinet platform by ½ in. to ¾ in. Place the Tilt'able underneath the machine so that the front of the machine is the same height as the cabinet surface. For extension tables, if yours is a Sew Steady Table (with black legs), you can order custom extension-table legs. For the Add-A-Table (with small gray or white legs), replace the bolt on the left rear leg with a 3-in. by ¼-in.-dia. carriage bolt with a slotted head (costing about 50 cents at a hardware store).

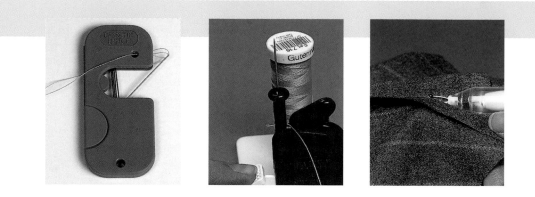

Needles
and

part SIX

Needles and threads are the most basic sewing supplies, but there are some innovative and creative variations of these everyday items that can make your sewing a little easier. Some of these have been around for a long time and some are brand new, but all add convenience.

Thread may be a humble topic, but specialty threads can make a difficult job much simpler. For example, elastic thread and fusible thread, available in most fabric stores, have particularly useful applications that you may not have even considered.

For those of us with less-than-perfect eyesight or hands that aren't surgeon-steady, there are a variety of foolproof needle threaders that will help you thread those needles having seemingly microscopic eyes. Once you get them prepared, a handy threaded-needle case can store your threaded needles neatly and knot-free, so they're ready when you are.

Threads

Fusible Thread

Lyla Messinger

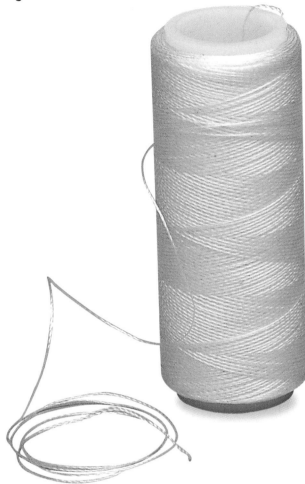

B inding a garment gives a finished, ready-to-wear look
that I love, but getting the look I
desire is often frustrating. I find that
using fusible thread with stretch knits
(including ribbing) cut on the crosswise grain, can make binding a
breeze. Thanks to a combination of
fusible elements and polyester, fusible
thread makes binding easy.

Fusible thread is used just like regular thread, but when heat, steam, and
pressure are applied to the stitched
area, the thread fuses with the fabric.

As a result, you can eliminate the
three most common problems inher-
ent to binding:

- twisting and slipping as the
  binding is being sewn

- not catching the binding's
  underside in spots

- producing an uneven width
  of the finished trim

Two of my favorite types are
ThreadFuse and Gutermann Fusible
Thread, because they are consistent in
quality and easy to fuse.

USING FUSIBLE THREAD

Fusible thread has a rough surface that makes it difficult to use in the needle; placing it in the bobbin of the sewing machine works much better. It's also important to use a longer stitch length when sewing with fusible thread, preferably a basting-length stitch. The more thread that lies on the surface of the fabric, the more easily it fuses.

Binding a garment with fusible thread

When binding garments, I have found that knit fabrics are simple to work with and the most forgiving for use as binding. In cases when woven fabric must be used, cut it on the bias grain for best results.

Note that varied seam widths may be used for different binding widths. A good rule of thumb is to make the trim approximately four times the seam width. This differs according to fabric because of the width needed to allow for turn of cloth. For example, a bulky fabric uses up more trim width to cover the edge of a garment. If this is the case, either add width to the trim or sew a narrower seam. Always experiment with the same fabric you'll be using in the garment. The technique is as follows:

1 Wind the fusible thread on the bobbin, and thread the machine; use regular thread on top.

2 With the fusible thread in the bobbin case, stitch 1½-in.-wide binding to the fabric edge, right sides

Fusible thread was used to sew the ribbed binding on the edges of this denim jacket.

Tip

When working with knit or bias binding, be careful to apply the trim to straight and slightly curved edges without stretching it. When working on sharp outside curves, use ease-plus when sewing the trim to the garment, because more fabric is required to cover the edge of the garment when the trim is turned to the inside. A sharp inside curve requires stretching the trim, because less fabric is required to cover the edge of the garment to allow the trim to lie flat. Practice on the same type of curve on your pattern.

together. Use a ⅜-in. seam and basting-length stitch.

3 At your ironing board, wrap the trim to the wrong side of the garment. Roll under the raw edge of the trim.

Binding the Fabric Edge

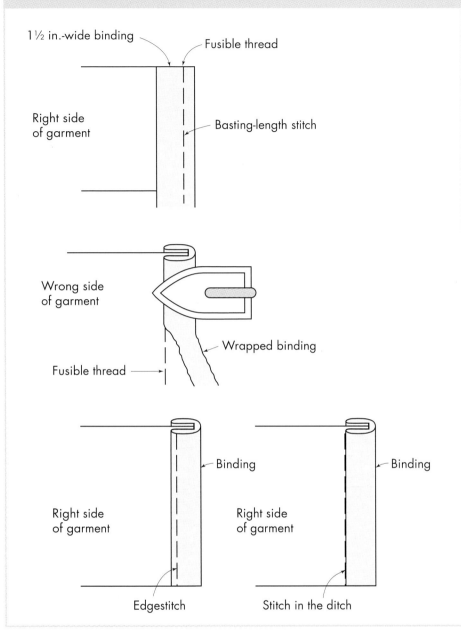

1½ in.-wide binding

Fusible thread

Right side of garment

Basting-length stitch

Wrong side of garment

Wrapped binding

Fusible thread

Binding

Binding

Right side of garment

Right side of garment

Edgestitch

Stitch in the ditch

4 Fuse small sections in place with the tip of the iron so the folded edge just covers the fusible thread. Continue until all the binding is fused in place.

5 From the right side of the fabric, edgestitch the trim close to the seam, or stitch in the ditch.

Tip

For ease of handling, use a fabric stiffener or spray starch to tame slippery or unruly fabrics before cutting or working with the strips. The stiffener will wash out when the task is complete.

Elastic Thread

Connie Long

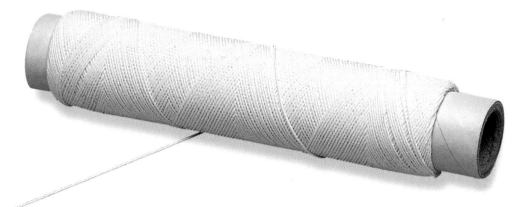

E lastic thread is typically woven or knitted into sweater hems to prevent the edges from stretching out and bagging. You can also use this thread to create elasticized smocking on lightweight fabrics. If you like to sew with a variety of knitted fabrics like I do, then you will find that elastic thread is perfect for sewing stable-yet-elastic buttonholes. It is also helpful to use elastic thread in the bobbin as a way to increase the elasticity of topstitched hems on bulky knits, as well as on knits that have a tendency to stretch out of shape when you topstitch the hem.

USING ELASTIC THREAD

To increase the elasticity and recovery of topstitched hems on bulky knits and ribbing, use polyester thread on top and elastic thread in the bobbin. Wind the elastic onto the bobbin by hand so that you don't stretch it, or use the machine to wind the bobbin without sliding the thread through the tension apparatus. Sew single- or multineedle straight-stitched hems without stretching the fabric as you sew. The straight stitch looks normal when relaxed but will have lots of stretch, and the stitches won't pop when you stretch the hem edge.

Elastic thread in the bobbin means that this straight-stitched hem on a bulky fabric won't pop.

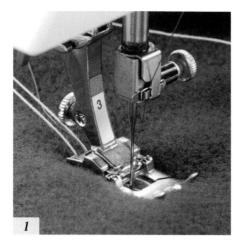

1

Elastic thread
for corded buttonholes

By using elastic thread instead of
gimp to sew corded buttonholes, you
can create stable-yet-elastic buttonholes that are perfect for knits. It is
important to sew over the elastic
thread without stitching through it, so
that the elastic can be pulled tighter
and adjusted to suit each fabric. How
you position and anchor the elastic
thread as you sew each buttonhole
will vary from machine to machine,
but you can always find a way to align
the thread so that you sew over the
thread without stitching through it.
The prong, hook, or toe will be either
in the front or the back of the presser
foot, depending on how your machine
sews buttonholes.

1 Position the elastic thread after
the needle is already inserted in the
fabric (it's easier this way). Start each
buttonhole with the needle centered,
and use the handwheel to lower the
needle into the fabric.

2 Hook the elastic thread over the
center prong at the front or back of
the presser foot, and take both elastic
ends under the presser foot while low-
ering it. Be sure the elastic thread is
able to slide under the presser foot so
that you don't sew through it when
sewing the buttonhole.

3 Sew the buttonhole.

4 Pull the elastic ends, and use a
coarse needle to bring them to the
back of the garment. Tie the ends to
maintain the buttonhole size, and cut
away any excess elastic.

Clover Needle Threader

Linda Lee

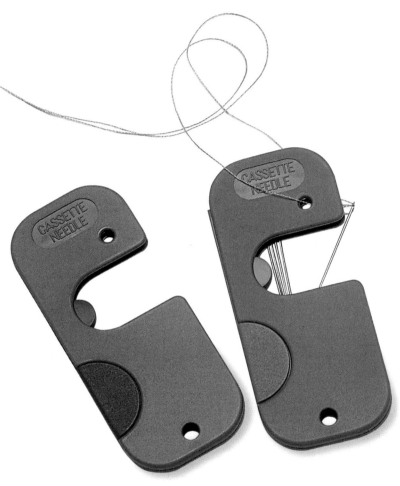

F or those times when you're taking a project on the road, a portable needle threader can be helpful. The Premier Needle Threading Cassette by Clover is a small, handy size that is easy to carry. This no-fail gadget is available either without needles or with small, medium, or large needles already included.

A standard wire needle threader, which holds about a dozen needles from sizes #2 through #10, fits neatly inside the case. Simply insert a strand of thread into a hole in the case (which also feeds through the concealed wire threader). When pulling a needle out of the case, it is automatically threaded. The only disadvantage is that you have to stop occasionally to feed more needles onto the threader.

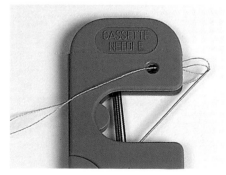

Lighted Seam Ripper and Needle Threader

Linda Lee

1 n certain circumstances, such as working on black fabric in poor light, I use the Lighted Seam Ripper and Needle Threader. The point and cutter on the seam ripper are not nearly as fine and sharp as the Clover ripper (see p. 49), but the real advantage is that the former comes with a built-in flashlight.

USING THE LIGHTED SEAM RIPPER AND NEEDLE THREADER

Two clear-plastic cones come with the tool, one with a seam ripper and the other with a needle threader, which fit over the end of the flashlight. When you click on the flashlight, the light shines through the clear-plastic cone, making it easy to remove stitches from dark fabrics or to thread needles. Two AAA batteries are required to operate the flashlight.

To remove stitches, simply insert the long prong under the stitch or between the seam. To use the needle threader, insert the wire loop through the eye of the needle, and put the thread through the wire loop. Pull the wire loop, and thread it back through the eye of the needle.

Ripping out seams in dark fabrics is much easier with a lighted seam ripper.

One-Step Needle Threader

Clotilde

T hreading needles can be frustrating and time consuming, especially for stitchers with "mature eyes." The solution is a piece of fine wire that is used as a needle threader. It was first used over 20 years ago to thread the very fine needles used in delicate Russian punch-needle embroidery. Today, this 4-in. length of very fine wire is still one of the best, threading any needle quickly and easily. Clotilde Inc. carries one step threaders, six to a package, which are conveniently placed on a magnetic strip to prevent accidental loss.

USING A ONE-STEP NEEDLE THREADER

To use the threader, simply insert thread into the large loop at the end. Then push the straight end effortlessly through the eye of any hand or machine needle for instant one-step threading.

This tool also saves time threading serger loopers. It goes through each looper and then on to thread the needle, all in one continuous motion. This is a time-saver when compared to other threaders, which must be backed out each time before proceeding to the next looper.

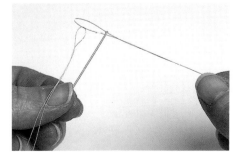

Dome Threaded-Needle Case

Clotilde

Q uilters find it annoying to continually rethread needles after every few minutes of quilting. It's much easier to have a series of needles that are threaded and ready to use. To solve this problem, Clover created the dome threaded-needle case. This small, portable case allows you to have threaded needles ready for instant use. It's not only ideal for quilters but for cross-stitchers too, since they are continually changing thread colors.

USING A DOME THREADED-NEEDLE CASE

The dome threaded-needle case holds 10 threaded needles ready to use, without any risk of tangling. To use the device, untwist the clear dome top and clip it onto the underside of the case. Then simply insert a threaded needle into any slot, letting the thread tail hang down into the crevice at the side. While gently holding the tail with one hand, rotate the blue slotted center with your other hand. As the device turns, it neatly coils up the thread tail and leaves no bothersome tangles.

Automatic Needle Threader and Cutter

Linda Lee

P oor eyesight and a lack of patience inhibit my ability to thread a needle the first time, every time. I've been on the hunt for the perfect needle threader for a long time, and I've finally found one of the best—the Automatic Needle Threader and Cutter. This threader is foolproof, even for the smallest eye size.

Formerly known as the Witch, this unusual gadget looks like it belongs in a museum. By its sheer design, I suspect that the threader has been around for a long time and has simply been repackaged for a newer audience. It's definitely not high tech, but it wins, hands down, in the category of best needle threader.

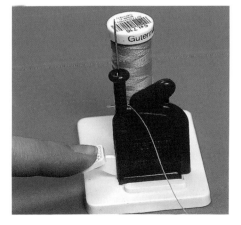

USING THE AUTOMATIC NEEDLE THREADER AND CUTTER

The automatic needle threader comes in two pieces, which need to be assembled. The white plastic base, which measures 1½ in. by 2½ in., has a spindle to hold a spool of thread and a channel into which fits a red plastic threading device. Lay the end of the spooling thread over an indentation on the device. Insert a needle of any size into the cylinder, with the eye pointing down. Then press down a white lever to push the threader wire through the eye of the needle. When you pull the needle out of the cylinder, it's threaded. A handy blade to cut the thread is located on the back of the device.

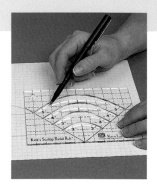  

Aids for
PRECISION

part SEVEN

ou've perfectly marked your fabric, cut it out precisely, and now you want to sew it with equal precision. Are there any notions out there that can help? You bet! Here are some of the most useful gadgets for measuring, pressing, turning, and getting a clearer view of what you're working on. These tools change tedious jobs into simple tasks, making your sewing more enjoyable as well as helping you produce better results.

Accurate measuring is so important for achieving consistent seam allowances, perfectly matched scallops, and elegant curves. All of these can be effortless with the right tools, and the range of specialized rulers is impressive. If you've ever wondered how the pros get those sharp-pressed and perfectly matched edges, templates are often the answer. With the help of these notions, you'll never worry about uneven patch pockets or a wavy hem again!

Hemming Template

Barbara Deckert

Measuring the depth of a hem every few inches, pinning it in place, and pressing the folded edge before you can even begin to sew takes forever, especially if you are hemming draperies or very full skirts. A hemming template makes this process fast and easy. One of the best is the Dritz Ezy-Hem Gauge.

It's a piece of metal about 8 in. by 4 in., with one curved edge and three straight ones. The longer curved edge is clearly marked with parallel lines at ¼ in., ⅝ in., 1½ in., 2 in., 2¼ in., and 2½ in. from the edge of the template; these hem depths are also converted into metric units. The flip side of the guide measures distances from the long straightedge.

USING A HEMMING TEMPLATE

The Ezy-Hem Gauge can be used to turn and press the edges before stitching in place; this is useful for pockets, belts and waistbands, pattern alterations, and even patches and appliqués. Use the template with a steam iron, but be careful; the gauge may be hot after pressing.

> **Tip**
>
> Be careful not to touch the bare metal of the template with your iron because it may scratch the iron's soleplate.

Here's how to use the Ezy-Hem Gauge:

1 For a straight hem, lay the long, straight side of the gauge over the wrong side of your fabric.

2 Fold the hem allowance over the guide, and line up your desired hem depth with the appropriate line on the template.

3 Press the hem right over the gauge.

For curved hems, stitch ¼ in. from the raw edge, using a basting stitch to ease the hem. Turn up the fabric along the desired hemline and insert the Ezy-Hem Gauge. Using a pin, pull up stitches every few inches until the hem lies flat, and then press.

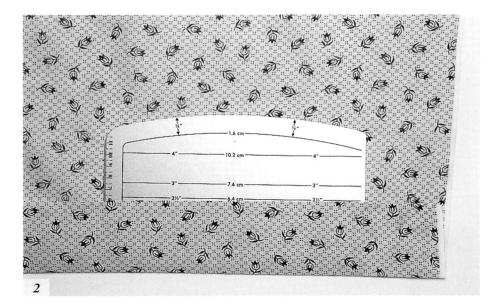

2

Pocket Curve Template

Clotilde

 dentical curves on patch pockets are critical for a professional-looking garment. The standard way to achieve smooth curves uses a time-consuming technique: sewing a row of gathering stitches around the curve, then drawing up the gathers to make it nicely rounded. Pockets can be made much more quickly, however, with the help of a Pocket Curve Template.

USING A POCKET CURVE TEMPLATE

This small metal plate has four curved corners, each with a slightly different shape; these curves can be used with almost any pocket pattern. Follow the instructions on the facing page for using the template:

1 Finish the hem at the top of the pocket.

2 Decide which curve you want to use. Place that curved corner on the seamline of your fabric pocket.

3 Slide the triangular-shaped clip underneath the fabric, bringing the seam allowance up and over the template, as shown.

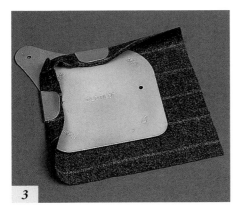

4 Lightly press the folded-up seam allowance in place.

5 Remove the template. Repeat this process for the second curve of the pocket.

6 Pin the pocket to your garment, and edgestitch it in place.

The template can also be used to achieve identical curves on collar bands and cuffs. Rather than eyeballing the stitching line, simply trace the desired curve from the template onto the edge of each collar band. Now you have a guideline to help you stitch perfectly matched curves.

Tip

To avoid possible slippage, use Wash-A-Way Wonder Tape or No-Pin Basting Fabric Adhesive to hold the pocket in place when stitching.

Scallop Radial Rule

Carol Ahles

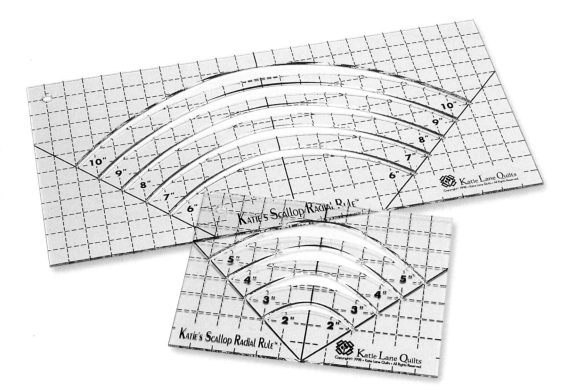

1 have always loved the look of appliqués, borders, and appliquéd, turned-edge scalloped hems, but I rarely did them because of the work involved in planning and drawing the scallops, as well as the difficulty in getting perfectly turned edges. Now, creating shaped, appliquéd hems has become surprisingly easy, thanks to the Scallop Radial Rule—a tool that helps you draw even and accurate scallops every time.

The Scallop Radial Rule and the Mini Scallop Radial Rule, both from Katie Lane Quilts, are very handy. The regular Rule has arcs in 1-in. increments, for tracing scallops 6 in. to

10 in. wide. The Mini Rule (which I use most often) is for scallops 2 in. to 5 in. wide. On both Rules, there is a shallower and a deeper version for each width.

USING THE SCALLOP RADIAL RULE

Always draw the scallops on paper first. Measure the hem depth from the bottom of the paper, and draw a horizontal line. Starting at one side, draw as many scallops on this line as will fit, using the Scallop Radial Rule. Keep in mind that shallow scallops are

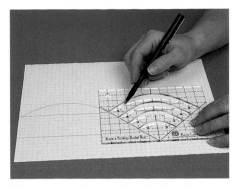

Choose the scallop depth and width that best suits your project.

It is much easier to have the dip of a scallop, not the point, centered on a seam. (This eliminates the problem of trying to have a perfect point at the bulk of a seam.) On a project with seams, such as a skirt, sew the skirt front to the skirt back at one side seam, and start tracing with the center (dip) of a scallop on that seam. If there is only one side seam, as on a pillowcase, press a crease halfway and start there.

easier to turn neatly and smoothly than deep ones. A pleasing scallop width (from point to point) will generally be narrower for smaller projects (for example, a toddler's dress or a small pillowcase) and wider for larger projects.

Once you've designed the right scallop depth and width for your project, it's time to transfer the scallops onto your fabric. I usually start with fabric wider than what the finished project requires and draw as many scallops as will fit, then cut off the excess. If this is not possible, measure the finished width (excluding seam allowances), and divide it by a pleasing scallop width for a project that size. This will give you the number of scallops that will fit. It will likely be a number with a fraction, so you may have to experiment with a slightly different scallop width, use scallops of varying widths, or fudge by slightly overlapping or spreading as you draw the scallops.

BABY'S (OR BOUDOIR) PILLOWCASE WITH CONTRASTING, SCALLOPED HEM

This beautiful baby's (or boudoir) pillowcase is surprisingly easy to make. It may be folded over to use as an elegant lingerie bag or personalized with additional hand or machine embellishment. The contrasting, scalloped, turned-edge hem is appliquéd with a machine stitch that closely resembles the hand pinstitch.

For this project, use an open-toe (appliqué) foot so that the edge of the appliqué is visible. Also, you may have to experiment with the stitch pattern as you try to anchor points securely with a stitch at or near the top. This project involves using a heat-resistant template product, Templar, which is also helpful in making accurate turned edges.

Materials

Light- to medium-weight, prewashed linen or cotton:
- for the pillowcase: 20 in. (or desired length) long by 32 in. wide
- for the shaped border: 3¼ in. long by 32 in. wide (contrasting color)

Templar
Stencil brush or Q-tip
Starch

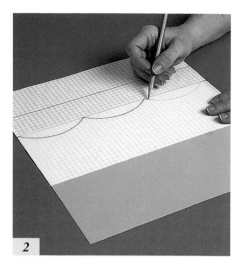

1 Spray-starch and press the border fabric without stretching it. Lightly crease at the center.

2 Use the Mini Scallop Radial Rule's shallow 4-in. arc to draw scallops onto the Templar with a sharp pencil, overlapping slightly for scallops no wider than 3¾ in. (The scallops on the pillowcase shown here are ¾ in. deep.) Then cut carefully along

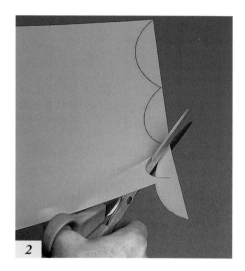

> **Tip**
>
> Start stitching on a straight or slightly curved area, such as the inside curve on a scallop, not on a point or at a seam.

this line, cutting off as much of the pencil marking as possible. Smooth any rough edges with an emery board.

3 Trace the scallops onto the border strip using the scalloped Templar as a template. To do this, unfold the border strip and trace the scallops along the top, aligning points just below the cut edge. Start at the creased center fold with the center (dip) of the scallop, and continue tracing scallops to one end.

4 Fold the fabric at the center. Cut through both layers at once, using scissors or a rotary cutter.

5 Trace the scallops along the lower strip, aligning the lower part of the curves about ¼ in. from the lower edge of the strip. Start again at the center fold with the center of the scallop and continue tracing scallops for the entire width. Align the lower scallops with those at the top. Do not cut the lower scallops. (If you wish, omit this step and make the lower edge straight.)

6 With the wrong side up (the lower scallop markings should be visible), align the scalloped Templar about ³⁄₁₆ in. below the cut-scalloped fabric edge.

7 Using a stencil brush or Q-tip, lightly dampen the fabric above the Templar with starch, one scallop at a time. Fold and press edges over the Templar, starting with the inside curve. Then press each side of the scallop over the Templar using the edge of the iron, creating neatly folded points. If any fabric extends over

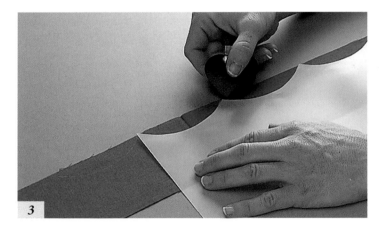

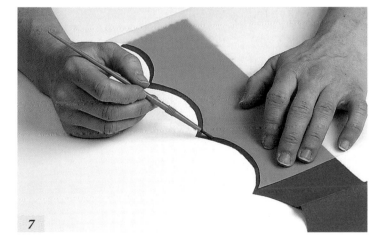

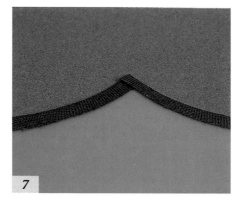

7

the point (as sometimes happens with the sharper points), dampen it with spray starch, fold it back, and press.

8 Spray-starch and press the lower edge of the pillowcase fabric. Stitch the right side of the border to the wrong side of the fabric, aligning the center creases.

9 Align the straight edges, and stitch along the traced scallop line. Use a straight stitch, length 1.5mm to 2mm, upper tension 4, 70U needle, and a basic or straight-stitch foot.

10 Trim to ⅛ in., and clip to within a few threads at the inner points.

11 Turn the border to the right side. Press, spray-starch, and press

> **Tip**
>
> To reduce puckering, slightly loosen (lower) the upper tension and try more spray starching and pressing and/or a lightweight tear-away stabilizer under the background fabric.

again. Use pins, a glue stick, or a temporary spray adhesive to hold the hem in place for stitching.

12 Fold it in half, aligning the scallops. Estimate the midpoint of the last scallops at the outer edges, and mark a line just less than ½ in. toward the edge from the estimated midpoint. Cut along this line through both layers and continue for the length of the pillowcase.

13 Pin and use a French seam to sew the side of the pillowcase, including the border. To make a French seam, first pin the wrong sides together. Adjust the folded border, if necessary, so it matches. Stitch a seam just less than ¼ in. wide, then press and trim to ⅛ in. Next, fold the right sides together. Stitch a seam just less than ¼ in. wide, and press.

14 Sew the end of the case with a French seam or other seam finish, such as a straight stitch or overcast. Trim and press.

15 Stitch the border in place with a handsewn-looking appliqué stitch of your choice. The sample shown here is stitched with the Parisian hemstitch (pinstitch), stitch length 2.4, width 1.5 to 2, using a 120/9 Universal needle, and fine machine-embroidery cotton threads. The forward and back stitches are on background fabric, and the zigzag swings just wide enough to catch the hem.

Magnetic Seam Guide

Sandra Betzina

W ithout exact ⅝-in. seam allowances, garment construction does not go smoothly. Collars don't fit necklines, sleeves don't fit armholes, and facings don't match up smoothly. Inaccurate seam allowances are prevalent among home sewers, but you can avoid this aggravation by using a magnetic seam guide. This simple tool keeps your seamlines exact every time, saving many a garment.

By guiding the fabric along its edge, a magnetic seam guide can help you stitch perfect seams and tucks without measuring.

USING A MAGNETIC SEAM GUIDE

The magnetic seam guide works just as its name implies. It is a power-grip magnet that adheres to the sewing machine, providing a straight-line guide for the fabric as you sew.

On many of the newer machines, the magnetic seam guide tends to slide around. If this happens on your machine, simply measure ⅝ in. to the right of the needle and make a scratch or mark a line with colored nail polish. Position the magnetic seam guide on the mark, and tape it into position. As you sew, simply allow the raw edge of the seam to touch the side of the magnetic seam guide. Now, all of your seams will be accurate.

Steam-A-Seam 2

Sandra Betzina

Steam-A-Seam 2 is a fusible web product with a paper liner. While this product has many uses, my favorite technique is to use it for flat, invisible hems on difficult fabrics, such as slinky knit and satin. Slinky knit grows when machine-hemming, so the Steam-A-Seam 2 acts as a stabilizer. On satin, it is useful as a form of underlining to which the hemstitch can be attached—the only way to achieve a truly invisible hem on satin. Steam-A-Seam 2 is nearly permanent; it can handle up to 37 wash-and-dry cycles as well as numerous dry cleanings.

USING STEAM-A-SEAM 2

For a flat, invisible hem with Steam-A-Seam 2, use the ½-in. width. (It's also available in a ¼-in. width.)

1 Roll off a length of ½-in.-wide Steam-A-Seam 2.

2 Finger-press the web side against a ½-in. hem allowance. The web is slightly sticky, so it will adhere to the hem allowance until you iron it in place.

3 With the paper still attached, iron lightly for 1 or 2 seconds.

4 Peel off the paper, and finger-press the hem in place. Because this side is also sticky, it will stay in place until you press.

5 Cover the surface with a press cloth. Press it into position with a dry iron on medium high temperature for 10 seconds. Hemming is now complete.

This product is also terrific for attaching facings to the underside of a garment and creating a permanent roll on a shawl collar. For these occasions, I use the ½-in. width.

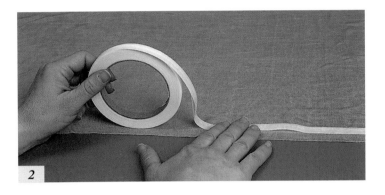

18-Inch Clear Ruler

Linda Lee

A ruler is an indispensable tool for me. I use it not only for measuring but as a straightedge for cutting and drawing. My favorite one is the 18-in. Quilt and Sew Ruler. Although it is marketed as a device for drafting any size patchwork or appliqué pattern, I use it as my primary tool for basic marking and measuring in my home-decorating and fashion sewing projects.

This slightly flexible, clear-plastic ruler is 2 in. wide and 18 in. long. It is ruled with graph lines in red permanent ink and marked in ¹⁄₁₆-in. increments, both horizontally and vertically. The same ruler is available with a protective metal edge for use with rotary cutters, but I prefer the original; its size, weight, and flexibility make it easy to handle.

USING AN 18-IN. CLEAR RULER

Often, I use the ruler in conjunction with a chalk marker to indicate perfect, straight lines for pressing and stitching, as well as for cutting with a rotary cutter. The 2-in. width is also perfect for cutting most bias strips.

Another handy use for the ruler is to enlarge or reduce patterns from magazines and other publications. For example, if the side of one square equals ½ in., you can use the ruler to prepare a block divided into a grid of ½-in. squares; you can then draw the design square by square.

For drawing circles and scallops, the Quilt and Sew Ruler has a zero-centering scale with holes pierced every ½ in. To draw a circle or scallop:

1 Draw a horizontal line as a guide.

2 Using the ruler, place a sharp pencil, heavy pin, or thumbtack in the hole marked 0 on the line.

3 Place a second pencil in the hole that represents half of the diameter of your finished circle.

4 To make a circle, rotate the ruler like a compass. To form a scallop, rotate the ruler in a semicircle, from one side of the line to the other. Remove the center pin while holding the pencil in place, and swing the ruler around so that the center hole is in position on the line for making the next scallop.

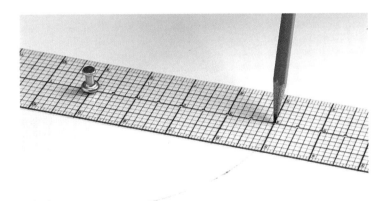

4

6-Inch Design Ruler

Carol Ahles

R ulers have innumerable uses in sewing. I usually keep a 6-in. design ruler close at hand for accurate measurements as well as a variety of other tasks. Besides simply measuring, the ruler can also be used for making patterns and pattern alterations, spacing buttonholes, measuring and finding foldlines for tucks and darts, and marking positions for all types of decorative detail, needlework, and trim.

The ruler is made of clear, see-through, flexible plastic and has measurements printed in inches and in centimeters. The printing is laminated, so it won't rub off, and has a center hole for pivoting plus additional holes for drawing arcs.

USING A 6-IN. DESIGN RULER

The ruler is particularly useful for making accurate scallops. In addition to the center hole, additional holes are marked with numbers showing the size of the scallop that can be made, up to 6 in. in diameter.

When drawing scallops, note that pivoting at the line representing the top of the hemline creates deep scallops that are difficult to fold under. Instead, draw a line on the graph paper for pivoting that is 1 in. to 2 in. above the top hemline. Experiment with different pivot lines and radiuses until you get the scallops you want. I usually put cardboard under the

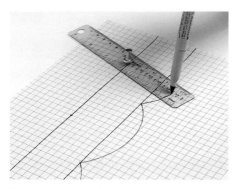

The three holes in the design ruler are useful for drawing accurate scallops.

graph paper, put a pin in the hole being used for pivoting, and use a different colored pen or pencil for each scallop size to make the scallops easier to distinguish.

I also like to use the design ruler to find the best marking on the needle plate and the best needle-position combination for the most common topstitching and seam allowances. Lower the needle into the center hole of the ruler (a large size—like a 120/19 Universal needle—will be the most accurate), then experiment with all the possible guides, needle positions, and markings for the best combinations. (Unless you want metric measurements, turn the ruler so that the inch markings are facing you.) Record the results on an index card and keep it near your machine, so that this information is always just a glance away.

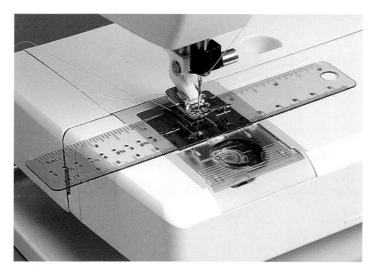

Use the design ruler with your sewing machine to find the best needle-position combination for common topstitching and seam allowances.

Magnifying Glasses

Gale Grigg Hazen

P inpoint accuracy is often necessary when sewing and making crafts. Whether you are hand-sewing needlecrafts such as cross-stitch, needlepoint, quilting, and appliqué, or using the sewing machine to make garments, crafts, or home-decorating projects, you must be exact while putting in stitches or taking them out. The only way to accomplish these tasks is to be able to see precisely, and magnifying glasses are one of the best ways to make things clearer.

TYPES OF MAGNIFYING GLASSES

- **Clip & Flip.** I wear reading glasses to sew, but I still find it difficult to see small areas, especially on dark colors. Even with glasses, tiny stitches can be incredibly hard to see. Clip & Flip attaches to your standard glasses to give you extra magnification, and it has crystal-clear acrylic lenses that won't distort images. Simply place them on the nosepiece of your glasses. When you need magnification, the lenses can be moved in place so that even the tiniest stitches can be seen clearly. When you don't need them, you can flip them up so they're out of your way. Clip & Flip also has a soft padded grip at the bridge and comes with a protective pouch for storage.

- **OptiVISOR.** This is an extremely accurate way to see any small area clearly. The headband is slightly cumbersome, but once it's adjusted, you can easily flip the magnifying lenses out of the way. The

OptiVISOR can be worn with or without your own glasses and comes with a detachable light. The biggest advantage to this type of magnifier is the ability to change the lenses, an option you may find helpful for close work or if your vision changes.

- **Hands-Free.** This type of magnifier is useful for people doing hand-sewing, needlecrafts, repairs, model-building, or any activity that requires both hands to be free. It sits on the chest and is held in place with a cord around the neck. This brand of magnifier has a clip-on, battery-operated light to increase your ability to see clearly.

- **MagniCraft.** This bar magnifier will help you see lines of instructions on needlework patterns, cross-stitch, recipes, and graphs. It has built-in magnets that hold down the paper if used on a metal surface (I use a small, inexpensive cookie sheet).

Tweezers

Gale Grigg Hazen

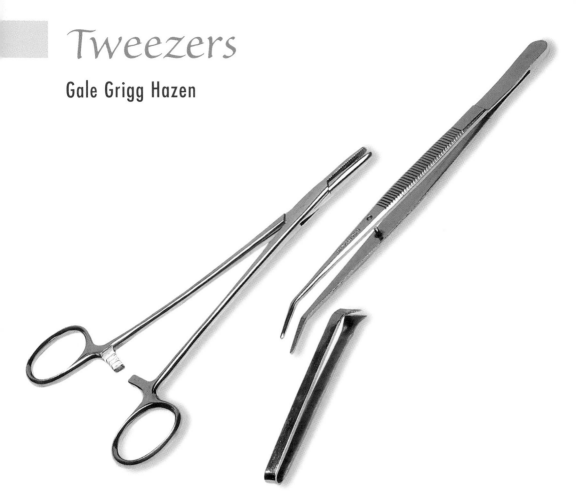

weezers can be invaluable when trying to remove small threads from fabrics. They are so useful that many brands of sergers include them as a standard accessory.

TYPES OF TWEEZERS

Tweezers come in different shapes and sizes, but all are wonderful, multipurpose tools.

- **Thread tweezers.** These small, sturdy tweezers are specifically designed to pull threads from fabric without damaging the fabric itself. For example, you can easily get hold of those tiny, knotted threads that remain when ripping out a seam. You can also use these tweezers to remove thread from a basted seam, which is especially hard to remove when it has been sewn over. Because their points are so sturdy, you can also use them to loosen and pull threads to the back of a seam in order to secure the seam with a knot.

- **Serger tweezers.** These multipurpose tweezers, one of my favorite tools, are 6¼ in. long and made of stainless steel. They have two important features. First, a pin on the inside of one tong goes through the other side, which supports the tips; this keeps them in line even when you squeeze

Serger tweezers are perfect for dealing with beads and other small objects on a sewing project.

them together with force. Second, the ridges on each side of the points create a nonskid grip on the thread or fabric you are trying to hold. These tweezers can be used to guide threads through hard-to-reach areas on the serger, or even to push thread through the eye of the needle. I also use serger tweezers when I am gluing and placing beads or other small objects.

- **Hemostats.** These tweezers are actually medical tools. They are very strong and have a set of overlapping, ridged bars between the handles that lock into place. The tweezers have several degrees of firmness and hold onto whatever is in the tips until the handle is released.

I've found that hemostats also have many uses in sewing. For example, they're perfect for inserting needles into hard-to-reach areas on your sewing machine or serger. They can also be used to turn small areas on tubes, pocket flaps, belts, or craft shapes. Insert the tips of the tweezers inside the object just to the length of the tweezers, and grab the fabric and pull. Repeat, if necessary, pulling the center out, using your other hand to smooth it down.

Tip

If there is a seam, catch all four layers in the pinch to reduce the chance of damaging the fabric.

Hemostats can be used to turn fabric tubes inside out, by grabbing small sections at a time with the tips.

resources

BEAR THREAD DESIGNS
Rte. 1, Box 1640
Belgrade, MO 63622
(573) 766-5695
Sew Clean

BELL'OCCHIO
8 Brady St.
San Francisco, CA 94103
(415) 864-4048
Horsehair braid, grosgrain ribbon

BONFIT AMERICA
8460 Higuera St.
Culver City, CA 90232
(800) 768-8008 Ordering
(800) 526-6348 Customer Service
(800) 208-8872 FAX
www.bonfit.com
No Hands! Elastic Wizard

BUTTONS 'N' BOWS
14086 Memorial Dr.
Houston, TX 77079
(281) 496-0170
Smocking pleater

CARSON OPTICAL
175A E. 2nd St.
Huntington Station, NY 11746
(800) 9-OPTICS
www.carson-optical.com
Clip & Flip, Hands-Free, MagniCraft

CC PRODUCT CO., INC.
71 Lawrence St.
Glens Falls, NY 12801
(800) 941-2181
(800) U-MAKE-IT
Tassel Magic

CLOTILDE
B3000
Louisiana, MO 63353-3000
(800) 772-2891 Ordering
(800) 545-4002 Customer Service
www.clotilde.com
Tatool, Perfect Pleater, No-Stick Sheet, press cloths, iron shoes, point presser, sleeve roll, hams, Velvet V Foot, One-Step Needle Threader, Pocket Curve Template, hemming template, Clo-Chalk, magnetic seam guide, Steam-A-Seam 2, Lighted Seam Ripper/Needle Threader, Tilt'able, No Hands! Elastic Wizard, Fiber-Etch, serger tweezers, fusible thread, sewing-machine feet, Scallop Radial Rule, Clover Quick Bias Fusible Tape, Clover Seam Ripper, Templar, Industrial Needle Board, OTT-LITE, magnifying glasses (including MagEyes Magnifier)

CLOVER
See Yo's Needlecraft and others

CROWNING TOUCH/FASTURN JUNCTION
3859 S. Stage Rd.
Medford, OR 97501
(800) 729-0280
www.fasturnjunction.com
Fasturn, Fastube Foot, Universal Presser-Foot Lifter

DONEGAN OPTICAL
15549 W. 108th St.
Lenexa, KS 66219
(913) 492-2500
OptiVISOR

ENVIRONMENTAL LIGHTING CONCEPTS, INC./OTT-LITE TECHNOLOGY
1214 W. Cass St.
Tampa, FL 33606
(800) 842-8848
(813) 626-8790 FAX
www.ott-lite.com
OTT-LITE

ERGONOMIC ADVANTAGE
3898 S. Jason St.
Englewood, Co 80110
(888) SEW-TILT
Tilt'able, SureFoot System

FISKARS MANUFACTURING CORP.
7811 W. Stewart Ave.
P.O. Box 8027
Wausau, WI 54402-8027
(800) 950-0203
(715) 842-2091
www.fiskars.com
Scissors, rotary cutters, shaped blades for rotary cutters

GINGHER
P.O. Box 8865
Greensboro, NC 27419
(800) 446-4437
(336) 292-6237
www.gingher.com
Scissors, pinking shears, duckbill scissors

GREENBERG & HAMMER
24 W. 57th St.
New York, NY 10019
(800) 955-5135
Professional tracing paper, horsehair braid, steel needle board, pressing hams, press cloths, iron shoes, point pressers, sleeve rolls, spiral-steel boning, scissors, rotary cutters, tracing wheels

HTC, INC.
103 Eisenhower Parkway
Roseland, NJ 07068
(973) 618-9380
www.htc-inc.net
*Tear-Away, wash-away, and
cut-away stabilizers*

HYMAN HENDLER AND SONS
67 W. 38th St.
New York, NY 10018
(212) 840-8393, -8394, -8395
Grosgrain ribbon

JO-ANN ETC.
Jo-Ann Fabrics
Hundreds of fabric/craft stores
across the country
www.joann.com

KATIE LANE QUILTS
P.O. Box 560408
Orlando, FL 32856-0408
(407) 855-2956 FAX
www.katielane.com
Scallop Radial Rule

L. J. DESIGNS
P.O. Box 21116
Reno, NV 89515-1116
(775) 853-2207
*Fusible Straight Stay Tape, Fusible
Bias Tape, Ultra-Soft Double Sided
Fusible Tape*

MARTHA PULLEN CO.
149 Old Big Cove Rd.
Brownsboro, AL 35741
(800) 547-4176
www.marthapullenco.com
Smocking pleater

NANCY'S NOTIONS
P.O. Box 683
Beaver Dam, WI 53916-0683
(800) 833-0690 Ordering
(800) 245-5116 Customer Service
www.nancysnotions.com
*Dome Threaded-Needle Case, One-
Step Needle Threader, Pocket Curve
Template, hemming template, Clo-
Chalk, magnetic seam guide, serger
tweezers, OTT-LITE, Universal
Presser-Foot Lifter, tracing wheels,
Tassel Magic, KK 2000, No Hands!
Elastic Wizard, presser feet, stabiliz-
ers, Templar, ThreadFuse, Fasturn,
clear elastic, Fiber-Etch, fusible stay
tape, 6-in. design ruler, Spinster*

ON THE SURFACE
P.O. Box 8026
Wilmette, IL 60091
(847) 675-2520
Tatool, Spinster

PROFESSIONAL SEWING SUPPLIES
P.O. Box 14272
Seattle, WA 98114-4272
(206) 324-8823
Chakoner

PRYM-DRITZ CORP.
P.O. Box 692
Spartanburg, SC 29304 0692
(800) 845-4948
(864) 576-5050
www.dritz.com
*Dritz Ezy-Hem Gauge, Quilt and
Sew Ruler, hemming templates,
magnetic seam guide, automatic
needle threaders, Rainbow Braid,
6-in. design ruler*

SEWING EMPORIUM
P.O. Box 5049
1079 Third Ave., Ste. B
Chula Vista, CA 91910
(619) 420-3490
(619) 420-4002 FAX
Velvet V Foot

SEW TRUE
447 W. 36th St.
New York, NY 10018
(800) 739-8783
(212) 947-9281 FAX
Press cloths, iron shoes

SILKPAINT CORP.
18220 Waldron Dr.
P.O. Box 18
Waldron, MO 64092
(800) 563-0074
www.silkpaint.com
Fiber-Etch

SOFTWEAR PRODUCTIONS, INC.
47 W. Polk St., #100-187
Chicago, IL 60605
(800) 297-9670
www.softwearproductions.com
*No Hands! Elastic Wizard, press
cloths, iron shoes, rotary cutters,
scissors, sewing-machine feet,
tweezers, needle threaders, bias
tape makers, OTT-LITE*

SPEED STITCH, INC.
3113 Broadpoint Dr.
Punta Gorda, FL 33983
(800) 874-4115
Sulky products

SULKY OF AMERICA
3113 Broadpoint Dr.
Punta Gorda, FL 33983
(800) 874-4115
www.sulky.com
Tear-Away, wash-away, and cut-away stabilizers; KK 2000

THAT PATCHWORK PLACE
Martingale & Co.
P.O. Box 118
Bothell, WA 98041-0118
(800) 426-3126
www.patchwork.com
Papers for foundation piecing

TOSCA CO.
13503 Tosca Lane
Houston, TX 77079
(713) 984-8545
Smocking pleater

THE WARM CO.
954 E. Union St.
Seattle, WA 98122
(206) 320-9276
www.warmcompany.com
Steam-A-Seam 2

YO'S NEEDLECRAFT
P.O. Box 11033
Carson, CA 90749
(310) 515-6473
(310) 518-2634
www.yosneedlecraft.com
Hera Marker, Clover Seam Ripper, needle threader, bias tape maker, thread tweezers, Quick Bias Fusible Tape, Pocket Curve Template

photo credits

Rodolphe Fouché: pp. 25–27

Scott Phillips, © The Taunton Press, Inc.: p. 77 (courtesy *Threads* magazine), p. 79 (top, courtesy *Threads* magazine), pp. 93–94, pp. 119–120, p. 140

Judi Rutz, © The Taunton Press, Inc.: cover, p. 8, p. 9 (left; right, courtesy *Threads* magazine), pp. 10–13, pp. 19–22, p. 24, p. 28, pp. 30–32, p. 34, pp. 36–39, pp. 42–44, pp. 46–51, pp. 53–57, pp. 60–69, pp. 72–76, p. 79 (bottom), pp. 80–81,

pp. 83–86, pp. 89–92, pp. 96–105, pp. 108–112, pp. 114–118, p. 121, pp. 123–126, pp. 128–132, pp. 136–137, p. 139, pp. 141–145, pp. 148–164, pp. 166–167

Jennifer Tarkington: p. 14, pp. 16–18

Laura White, © The Taunton Press, Inc.: p. 87 (courtesy *Threads* magazine)